The Doctors' Dinner Party

LETTER FROM THE GENERAL EDITOR

The Library of Arabic Literature makes available Arabic editions and English translations of significant works of Arabic literature, with an emphasis on the seventh to nineteenth centuries. The Library of Arabic Literature thus includes texts from the pre-Islamic era to the

LIBRARY OF
المكتبة
ARABIC
العربية
LITERATURE

cusp of the modern period, and encompasses a wide range of genres, including poetry, poetics, fiction, religion, philosophy, law, science, travel writing, history, and historiography.

Books in the series are edited and translated by internationally recognized scholars. They are published in parallel-text and English-only editions in both print and electronic formats. PDFs of Arabic editions are available for free download. The Library of Arabic Literature also publishes distinct scholarly editions with critical apparatus.

The Library encourages scholars to produce authoritative Arabic editions, accompanied by modern, lucid English translations, with the ultimate goal of introducing Arabic's rich literary heritage to a general audience of readers as well as to scholars and students.

The publications of the Library of Arabic Literature are generously supported by Tamkeen under the NYU Abu Dhabi Research Institute Award G1003 and are published by NYU Press.

Philip F. Kennedy
General Editor, Library of Arabic Literature

About this Paperback

This paperback edition differs in a few respects from its dual-language hardcover predecessor. Because of the compact trim size the pagination has changed. Material that referred to the Arabic edition has been updated to reflect the English-only format, and other material has been corrected and updated where appropriate. For information about the Arabic edition on which this English translation is based and about how the LAL Arabic text was established, readers are referred to the hardcover.

The Doctors' Dinner Party

by

Ibn Buṭlān

translated by

Philip F. Kennedy and Jeremy Farrell

foreword by

Emily Gowers

volume editor

Shawkat M. Toorawa

NEW YORK UNIVERSITY PRESS

New York

NEW YORK UNIVERSITY PRESS
New York

Please contact the Library of Congress for Cataloging-in-Publication data.

ISBN: 9781479827480 (paperback)
ISBN: 9781479827503 (library ebook)
ISBN: 9781479827473 (consumer ebook)

This book is printed on acid-free paper, and its binding materials are chosen for strength and durability. We strive to use environmentally responsible suppliers and materials to the greatest extent possible in publishing our books.

Series design and composition by Nicole Hayward
Typeset in Adobe Text

Manufactured in the United States of America

10 9 8 7 6 5 4 3 2 1

Hilary Ballon
In memoriam

Contents

Abbreviations

c.	century
ca.	circa = about, approximately
cf.	*confer* = compare
d.	died
ed.	editor, edition, edited by
EI2	*Encyclopaedia of Islam*, Second Edition
EI3	*Encyclopaedia of Islam Three*
fl.	flourished
MS, MSS	manuscript, manuscripts
n.d.	no date
n.p.	no place
no.	number
pl.	plural
Q	Qur'an
r.	ruled
vol., vols.	volume, volumes

Acknowledgments

The Library of Arabic Literature, now in its tenth year of publishing, would not have become what it is today without the support of the New York University Abu Dhabi Research Institute and Tamkeen. We can never tire of expressing our deepest gratitude to both entities for their funding of LAL with a generous grant.

This project would not have come to exist without the unstinting support and encouragement of Mariët Westermann, vice-chancellor of NYU Abu Dhabi; John Sexton, president emeritus of New York University; and, in particular, the late and much-lamented Hilary Ballon, deputy vice-chancellor of NYU Abu Dhabi until her passing away in 2016.

This book owes more than can be quantified to Chip Rossetti, Lucie Taylor, and James Montgomery, in their various capacities. Shawkat Toowara was the project editor, and his dauntingly erudite editorial skills saved this book from many infelicities. We have been graced in our work by his—and the executive reviewer's—enthusiasm, energy, and editorial acuity. In addition, Keith Miller and Stuart Brown have been assiduous in their copyediting and typesetting, respectively.

The book has also benefited from the scholarly interventions of a number of our colleagues, in particular Julia Bray, Gideon Dollarhide, Margaret E. Gaida, Bilal Orfali, Maurice Pomerantz, and Ignacio Sánchez. It is hard to find words to represent our gratitude for their patience, pertinent suggestions, and advice. Ignacio has been particularly generous in sharing his deep and wide-ranging knowledge of the works of Ibn Buṭlān. Most importantly, I thank Jeremy Farrell, a brilliant young scholar of medieval Islamic society. Such was his contribution that he is credited as a translator. It has been a real pleasure to work in close cooperation with this gifted social historian and scholar.

Philip Kennedy
New York City
April 2022

Foreword

EMILY GOWERS

The doctor at the banquet has been a literary fixture ever since Eryximachus was invited to Plato's *Symposium* and cured Aristophanes' attack of hiccups while contributing his own speech on love. What better guest than an expert in bodily well-being, whose solid input might tether airy philosophical conversations on the meaning and practice of the good life? The question remains: are this person's interventions sane, relevant, and conducive to health and happiness? Our "diet" may come from Greek *diaeta*, way of life, but one man's sensible nutritionist is often another's unhinged crackpot.

Eryximachus is a typically pompous representative of his profession. He rules against excessive drinking and musical entertainment, and the high-minded discussion about erotics—for him, the art of filling and emptying the body harmoniously, like medicine—is his idea. In less rarefied Greco-Roman contexts, practical advice on how to fill the stomach was commonly given, if not always taken seriously. Among the self-appointed wellness pundits—culinary, philosophical, legal—suffered by Horace in his second book of *Satires* (1st c. BC), a rustic sage, Ofellus ("Meatball"), discourses on radishes and bitter leaves as a healthy alternative to mullet and peacock, and an urban gourmet, Catius, promotes seafood and sorrel as the latest cures for sluggish digestion. Together with jurists, philosophers, and grammarians, Athenaeus includes the real-life doctor and dietary guru Galen as a character in his *Deipnosophistae*, "Sophists at Dinner" (3rd c. AD), an encyclopedic repository of learned contributions on everything dinner-related, from prostitutes to perfume to fish.

But a doctor in the house is not always a benign or even a reputable presence. Usually, when he brings bodily functions to the table, it is not so much to reassure the other guests as to force on them unwelcome, even disgusting encounters with the mechanics of digestion, evacuation, and other internal processes. Often, he is pedantic, in love with his discipline; sometimes, he is positively disruptive, as if he has forgotten his own guidance on self-regulation. Later examples in this vein include the out-of-control physician who subjects Tobias Smollett's Peregrine Pickle (1751) and his fellow-travellers to the repulsive flavors of a recreated Roman banquet, and Mel, the haunted cardiologist who completes a quartet of gin-drinkers in Raymond Carver's short-story version of the *Symposium*, "What We Talk About When We Talk About Love" (1981). What Mel chooses to talk about includes the attempted suicide by rat poison of his wife's abusive ex-partner and the "multiple fractures, internal injuries, hemorrhaging, contusions, and lacerations" he once witnessed in the elderly victims of a motorbike accident.

Events are bound to become more fractious when *all* the dinner-companions are doctors, including the host. This is the absurdist scenario of Ibn Buṭlān's *The Doctors' Dinner Party*, which starts, like Plato's *Symposium*, with a chance meeting, in this case in the Turkish city of Mayyāfāriqīn, in the early 11th century AD. With the narrator in tow (a Baghdadi doctor, like Ibn Buṭlān himself, but gullible and ignorant), the host invites an oculist, a phlebotomist, and a surgeon to ruminate with him on the state of modern medicine, while feeding them on little more than words. The meal is as dysfunctional as the Red Queen's dinner: unappetizing appetizers (vinegar and bitter chicory) are swiftly whisked away only to be replaced by a juicy lamb all of whose cuts, save the trotters, come with a stern health warning. The final course is a hideous display of medical instruments: pincers, lancets, catheters, hemorrhoid hooks, and saws for amputation. When the host falls asleep, his guests descend with relief on the food they have been denied.

Perhaps the closest classical equivalent of this savage parody of hospitality and collective dietary wisdom is the joyless feast served up to vengeful diners at the end of Horace's *Satires*: another performance of dissatisfaction. At a more basic level, the "Seven Sages" fresco from Ostia, the ancient port of Rome, shows Solon, Thales and other early Greek philosophers pooling lavatorial maxims ("Solon rubbed his belly to shit well"; "Thales said, if it's not easy, strain"; "Cunning Chilon taught how to fart silently") while squatters in a nearby latrine emit subversive slogans of their own: "Avoid wordy advice by using the sponge on a stick"; "Crap well and bugger the doctors." There is also more than a whiff of Petronius's millionaire ex-slave Trimalchio, who voices the same suspicion of medics when he over-shares his bowel habits and exercises surreal sleight of hand and a tyrant's whims over the guests he should be feeding nutritiously.

Galen had died in 216 AD, Hippocrates nearly 600 years earlier. But the reverential name-dropping in our text is a reminder that the medieval Arabic school of medicine was still firmly based on Greek principles: above all, on the Hippocratic system of "humors," the four bodily fluids that required careful calibration with regular purges, cupping, and bloodletting. Pythagorean and Platonic teachings are adapted here to the pulsing rhythms of the oud, the lute brought along by one of the doctors. Composed of "four natures," this is surrogate medical tool, spiritual salve, and bodily microcosm all at once (its strings are compared to veins and nerves, its plectrum to a scalpel). Well-tempered systems of diet, medicine, music, and philosophy were similarly juxtaposed in classical thought. Like the host's offering of wine "with ten benefits," the oud recalls the *tetrapharmacon* ("four-in-one drug"), a well-known Greek panacea which gave its name (jokingly) to a Roman imperial dish of sow's udder, pheasant, wild boar, and ham in pastry and (more seriously) to the "chief doctrines" of Epicurean philosophy.

At the doctors' dinner, the prevailing mood is melancholy. The host wistfully recalls not just pillars of the Greek past but also his more recent forebears. The golden age of medical expertise is gone, he laments, succeeded by an era of unqualified charlatans: "The spinal column of our profession has been severed." There is something a little fraudulent about this maudlin post-mortem. Could it be a sign that medicine is all too efficient when plagues are thin on the ground and the usual supply of fresh corpses, which used to arrive at the graveyards "like flowers in bloom," has dried up? Or does he simply envy those of his colleagues who have sold out to luxury, their heads turned by a pretty face or tuneful melody when they should be researching "opacities in Hippocrates and Galen; solar and lunar cycles; and pulses"? Physicians who used to drink from puddles now feed on delicately peeled broad beans and finely strained eggplant. The host's threnody rings false when the medical profession, while battered by controversy, is obviously in such fine fettle.

It is more likely that the host is heir to the *doctores inepti* of classical literature, experts (in any field) who are far less competent than they pretend to be. Especially when he claims startlingly that it is a good idea to prescribe laxatives for diarrhea, and better for the health to be anxious than calm. The Greco-Syrian satirist Lucian (2nd c. AD) is probably our richest ancient source for bogus and unconventional doctors. These include such memorable figures as the "false prophet" Alexander of Abonoteichos, who invented a panacea involving goat's fat; two doctors from Damascus who hoard a secret remedy for gout; a quack who promotes cough medicine but succumbs to violent paroxysms himself; and Sopolis, who purges Lexiphanes of the pretentious verbiage that is clogging him. The narrator of one Lucianic dialogue (*Philopseudes*, "Lover of Lies") in which miracle cures for gout are hotly debated ends up wishing he could take an emetic in order to eliminate everything he heard there. When his host complains about students who fail to take in medical information, Ibn Buṭlān may be hinting that *The*

Doctors' Dinner Party will have a similar effect on his readers: they will either absorb nothing or leave bloated.

The story's local color is all its own, from the puffed-up physicians who strut about in "turbans and toques, capes and seal rings," twisting the waxed ends of their moustaches, to the town's dusty, aromatic apothecaries' stores, with their "rows of earthenware pots, ornamental trays . . . dark painted doors, scales, measures, sieves, filters, and washbasins . . . henna, rosewater, dark dyes, zinc sulphate, laxatives and Mary Mother's incense." A delectable illustration from a Mamluk manuscript of the text (dated 672/1273) shows turbaned doctors guzzling around a low table, as trays of jewel-colored fruit and wine float above their heads and the host awakes irate from his quilted sleeping bag. Even so, *The Doctors' Dinner Party*, with its affectionate mistrust of the profession—its grandiosity, mysterious doctrines, and practical ineptitude—belongs unmistakably to a broader Mediterranean tradition of anti-medical satire.

Emily Gowers
University of Cambridge

Introduction

The Author

Al-Mukhtār ibn al-Ḥasan ibn Buṭlān was born in the early part of the fifth/eleventh century, probably in Baghdad. In all likelihood a Nestorian Christian,[1] he was the star student of the most celebrated philosopher-doctor of the first half of the eleventh century, the Nestorian priest Abū l-Faraj Ibn al-Ṭayyib (d. ca. 434/1043). Ibn al-Ṭayyib was a prolific writer and teacher of medicine, philosophy, and logic, and many of his voluminous writings were commentaries on the Aristotelian corpus.[2] This depth of knowledge had a great influence on Ibn Buṭlān, who became a polymath in his own right.

Ibn Buṭlān's most famous work is his *Almanac of Health* (*Taqwīm al-ṣiḥḥah*), a medical work composed ca. 437/1046, which garnered him fame in the Latin West until the early sixteenth century. A German translation produced in Strasbourg in 1533 followed several Latin translations of the work, all entitled the *Tacuinum Sanitatis*. Its organizational framework, within a scheme of Galenic humoral medicine, was as important and innovative as were its contents, which he arranged in tables, probably under the influence of earlier astronomical works. These tables represent the broad essentials of a healthy life, ranging from hygiene and dietetics to environment and exercise.

Other than his training with Ibn al-Ṭayyib, we know little about Ibn Buṭlān's life in Baghdad before 440/1049. From his writings, it is clear that he immersed himself in the study of a wide variety of topics, including astronomy, physiognomy, Galenic medicine, philosophy, logic, and the welfare of monks. We do know that he was closely associated with the ʿAḍudī hospital in Baghdad (constructed in 370/981). Hospitals at this time were not just places where the sick were treated, but, like their modern counterparts, also venues for medical instruction and where doctors effectively bolstered their credentials.

In the late winter of 440/1049, a few years after the death of his mentor Ibn al-Ṭayyib, Ibn Buṭlān left Baghdad and headed for Cairo, which he reached in the late autumn. His eventful journey was an opportunity for social observations. He eventually wrote a travelogue, which he dedicated and sent to Hilāl al-Ṣābiʾ (d. 448/1056), a close patron in Baghdad. The work does not survive, but was incorporated into *The Book of Spring* (*Kitāb al-Rabīʿ*) by Hilāl's son, Ghars al-Niʿmah (fl. fifth/eleventh c.), which in turn survives in Ibn al-Qifṭī's (d. 646/1248) lengthy entry on Ibn Buṭlān in his mostly medical prosopography, *The History of Scientists* (*Tārīkh al-ḥukamāʾ*). The geographer Yāqūt al-Ḥamawī (d. 626/1229) also quotes it in his entries about the northern Levant in *The Dictionary of Places* (*Muʿjam al-buldān*).

En route to Cairo, Ibn Buṭlān made stops in Raḥbah, Ruṣāfah, and Aleppo, where he had a lengthy stay and where the Mirdasid emir Muʿizz al-Dawlah (d. 454/1062) is said to have asked him to identify the ideal location for the foundation of a hospital. Abū Dharr al-Ḥalabī (d. 884/1479) quotes a legend that Ibn Buṭlān did so by hanging meat all over Aleppo to determine where it would remain the least putrefied and selected that spot for the hospital.[3] After Ibn Buṭlān humiliated Abū l-Khayr al-Mubārak ibn Sharārah (d. ca. 490/1097), an influential Aleppan Christian, in a public debate, the latter hounded him out of town. As we will see, this was not the last time he would make himself unpopular with a local leader and his community. He next traveled to ʿImm, then on to Antioch, which he adored (perhaps because it was the birthplace of Ibn al-Tayyib); Laodicea (Latakia); and Jaffa.

There is little doubt that Ibn Butlān made the trip to Cairo in order to seek out the famous physician Ibn Riḍwān (d. 453/1061). He was already aware of Ibn Riḍwān's often polemical compositions about Galenic humoral medicine, books that criticized the works of others; notoriously, he had attacked both Ḥunayn ibn Isḥāq and Ibn al-Ṭayyib for their supposed faulty grasp of Galenism. Ibn Riḍwān was a powerful figure, and Ibn Buṭlān hoped for a reception in Cairo that would boost his flagging career prospects.

Ibn Buṭlān's first meeting with Ibn Riḍwān, at the palace of a Fatimid minister, was amicable and professionally courteous, but when Ibn Riḍwān showed little sign of promoting Ibn Buṭlān to the position to which he aspired, Ibn Buṭlān made the mistake of writing an open letter to the medical community of Cairo. It was not an ad hominem attack, but he did make remarks that incensed Ibn Riḍwān, especially in the criticism he leveled against one al-Yabrūdī, a Damascene physician who had published a treatise stating that the body temperature of a bird's hatchling is warmer than that of a chicken's. The debate had its roots in Greek natural science; Ibn Buṭlān maintained that movement produces heat, and since the young chicken moves about independently immediately upon hatching whereas a young bird is helpless, the young chicken has the warmer constitution.[4] There was no real cause for Ibn Buṭlān to devote so much space to the subject in an open letter, other than an appetite for controversy.

Ibn Riḍwān's reply was vitriolic, accusing Ibn Buṭlān of being a mediocre doctor (*mutaṭabbib*) and an improperly trained physician (*ṭabīb*). This triggered a defensive and detailed reply by Ibn Buṭlān in which he called into question the very nature of Ibn Riḍwān's training, pointing out in blunt terms that proper training as a doctor came from reading widely under the tutelage of an elder mentor who could correct one's mistakes and misapprehensions about medicine: Ibn Riḍwān was entirely self-taught. Ibn Riḍwān wrote four more letters in response, two of which survive, including one in which he advises all the doctors of Cairo to shun the pretentious visitor.

Ibn Buṭlān was obliged as a result of these intemperate exchanges to leave Cairo never to return, his hopes for advancement there stymied by his own rashness. Interestingly, religion—Ibn Riḍwān was Muslim, Ibn Buṭlān Christian—appears to have played no part in the poisonous correspondence between the two men.

Sometime before 445/1054, Ibn Buṭlān returned the way he had come, but he turned westward after Antioch and headed for Constantinople. Michael Cerularius, the Patriarch of Constantinople, commissioned him to write a treatise about the use of unleavened bread in the Eucharist.[5] His successful handling of such a weighty theological matter was as impressive as his medical knowledge, and on both counts he was subsequently held in high esteem.[6] Significantly, this was a time of great contention between the two churches of Rome and Byzantium, and they split in that same year. The year 1054 is also when plague struck the Byzantine capital and spread across the Near East. This is significant in the context of *The Doctors' Dinner Party*. When Ibn Buṭlān describes, fictitiously but feasibly, a town in northern Syria as completely cleansed of plague, it must therefore have been sometime before 1054. We believe this supports the argument that Ibn Buṭlān composed *The Doctors' Dinner Party* during his time in Cairo, or even before he arrived there, as the first of two works partly reflecting his contretemps with the irascible Ibn Riḍwān.

Once he left Constantinople, Ibn Buṭlān spent the rest of his life in and around Aleppo and Antioch. The latter became his favorite town, and was where he supervised the construction of a hospital. In a life rich in its diversity of interests, he had dealings with some of the luminaries of his time, mourning those who died during the plague years, including the jurist and high government official al-Māwardī (d. 450/1058) and the blind poet al-Maʿarrī (d. 449/1057), who was a close friend. Toward the end of his life he became a monk and retired to a monastery. He died in 458/1066. The Aleppan antipathy toward Ibn Buṭlān appears to have survived after his death, since it was said there that his tomb was strangely cursed: any lamp lit in its vicinity was immediately, spontaneously, and supernaturally extinguished.

Medicine in the Early Islamic World

The tradition of medieval Islamic medicine Ibn Buṭlān inherited was the Greek and Hellenistic humoral tradition—that is, the teachings of Hippocrates that were later refined, developed, and documented in the writings of Galen of Pergamum. These were translated into Syriac and Arabic, notably by Ḥunayn ibn Isḥāq (d. 260/873–74), whose son Isḥāq ibn Ḥunayn (d. 298/910), also a physician and translator, is mentioned in *The Doctors' Dinner Party*. The Galenic system was then developed by the Arab physicians of the third/ninth to the sixth/twelfth centuries,[7] most of whom were either Christian, from the Nestorian community in large part, or Jewish.[8] The Nestorian Bukhtishūʿ family, for instance, originally from Gondeshapur, became a byword for Galenic medical practice: eight successive generations served the Abbasid caliphs. One member of that family, Jibrīl ibn Bukhtīshūʿ (d. 247/861), appears in *The Doctors' Dinner Party* in an exchange he is said to have had with the caliph al-Maʾmūn (r. 199–218/815–833; d. 218/833) about the latter's teeth, and is mentioned in verses by Abū Nuwās (d. ca. 199/815).

Earlier medicine from the second/eighth to the third/ninth century had to some extent become pluralistic, absorbing pre-Islamic and early Islamic folklore, much of it based on local practice and available natural medicines, as well as some elements of Indian, Persian, and Zoroastrian customs. Prophetic medicine (*al-ṭibb al-nabawī*), a corpus of prescriptive ordinances based on local practice and materia medica attributed to the Prophet, had obvious authority but was not a fully developed system.[9] In the main, medicine was founded upon the tradition of Galen, and Aristotelian and Greek philosophy in general were built into the system, hence the references in *The Doctors' Dinner Party* to such figures as Hippocrates, Galen, and Dioscorides. It was only in the sixth/twelfth century that Ibn Sīnā's *Canon* became central to Islamic medicine, having been ignored for almost two centuries. His presence is hardly felt in *The Doctors' Dinner Party*, though he might be the one referred to in 10.18 as the "Persian sage."

By the eighth/fourteenth century, with the work of Ibn Taymiyyah (d. 661/1263), al-Dhahabī (d. 672/1274), and later al-Suyūṭī (d. 848/1445), prophetic medicine was consolidated in compendia. Practitioners were men of religion, not physicians properly speaking, and they relied on the authority of the sources of prophetic hadith, not the leverage of their own names. The point seems to have been to counter, or at least balance, the authority of Galenic medicine by showing that the Prophet had had recourse to doctors. These corpora were not meant to be in opposition. *The Doctors' Dinner Party* disparages only the so-called temple medicine, a term borrowed from the Greek, and the customs of the common people.

The Work

The plot of *The Doctors' Dinner Party* is simple, belying the sophistication of the work. The narrator, a young man, appears in the town of Mayyāfāriqīn, in the Diyār Bakr region that straddles western Anatolia and northern Syria. He has traveled there on foot from Baghdad, destitute and seeking work as a physician. He soon encounters an older man in the marketplace, who eloquently and courteously receives him and, after a brief discussion, invites him home for a meal. The young stranger claims he has an ailing stomach and will not be able to eat. This is central to the old fellow's invitation, for he turns out to be an atrocious miser, and a dinner guest who cannot consume food is a glorious find for a miser in search of company.

At the old fellow's house, a series of dishes are presented by a servant boy to the two men; in each case the host warns of the dangers of an unhealthy diet. The evening conversation begins with a sensible discussion that draws on the sayings of the ancient Greeks. The back-and-forth is odd but lucid. The narrator, who has now built up an appetite, gradually resists the old fellow's call for restraint. And when he shows little sign of heeding the advice of his austere host, the latter begins to show irritation. This change of tone becomes increasingly pronounced as the narrative progresses.

When the old fellow invites four medical specialists (a surgeon, a young phlebotomist, an apothecary, and an oculist) to join the "party" in order to partake of wine and song, and eventually, by turns, to test the young visitor about his medical knowledge, a parody ensues: the narrator cannot answer serious and pseudo-serious medical questions designed to distinguish genuine doctors from quacks. The host's mood and animus grow steadily more aggressive toward the young man, who admits, in four well-choreographed stages, to being unqualified in any of the medical disciplines. All the while, the wine has begun to turn the head of the now-cantankerous host. After a final bilious and rambling account about an "appalling" young charlatan, the general demise of medicine, and the ingratitude of people toward physicians, the old fellow falls into a stupor.

The old fellow wakes up in the penultimate scene to find that the young apprentice, together with the servant boy and the young stranger, have polished off most of the dishes and delicacies, a veritable feast that was scarcely touched during the initial grotesquely abstemious dinner. The "dinner party" ends with a vitriolic tirade by the old man against the "greedy," deceitful, and ungrateful young visitor. When the latter, in an epilogue of sorts, returns to the house a few days later—why, we cannot say exactly: was he being innocent or mischievous with his return to the premises, and what could he have expected would happen?—the host closes the window on him in a fit of indecorous pique. This petulant act is the very antithesis of proverbial Arab hospitality, which had been vaunted in some of the verses the old fellow cited at the beginning of the dinner.

The poetics of *The Doctors' Dinner Party* can be discerned from its rhetorical figures and the richness of language, imagery, and use of metaphor; its structure, grounded in a movement of crescendo; its contrasts, antitheses, and inversions; and the way it draws on a number of textual influences, notably the interplay of genres of writing, both poetic and prosaic. The crescendo is as much psychological as it is a narrative feature. Indeed, the psychology of the text is fascinating. We can posit what we might call a circumscribed, at times erotic, phenomenology of inebriation; this drives the narrative and the unfolding of a rich, farcical, and pseudoscientific dialogue.

Though the opening line forges an explicit connection with the celebrated *Kalīlah and Dimnah*, this does not mean *The Doctors' Dinner Party* is a collection of animal fables. Ibn Buṭlān is simply evoking what Ibn al-Muqaffaʿ states at the outset of his work: "Because such a book combined entertainment with wisdom, the wise would study it for its wisdom, and the simple for its value as entertainment."[10] Ibn Buṭlān was an erudite and literary-minded doctor, with broad, polymathic interests, as is reflected by this citation and by his abundant and apposite quotations from the classical tradition. In an aphorism he appears to borrow from *Kalīlah and Dimnah*—the image of the silkworm, which leaves life steadily behind the more it weaves its product, just as the sick suffered the same consequence in living their lives (§2.3)—he displays also his sensitivity to context.

The Doctors' Dinner Party, which comes across as facetious, satirical, and parodistic, with elements of burlesque and farce, is a relatively protracted piece of fiction. One might call it a novella in modern terms, though it is perhaps better understood as a short roman à clef.[11] Some modern scholars, following Ibn al-Qifṭī (d. 646/1248), have been too quick to identify it as a *maqāmah*, a prosimetric literary genre that often features con men and dupes. It has some features of the *maqāmah*, such as the use of rhyming prose (*sajʿ*) in a third-person narrative, and deceitful characters, hiding truths only to be gradually unmasked in different ways, but it is much longer and more complex than any single *maqāmah*. *The Doctors' Dinner Party* has also been labeled an autobiography. It almost certainly is not that, though it does have autobiographical elements shared across one or two of the composite characters.[12] The author himself calls it an epistle (*risālah*), and it does have a dedicatee, as epistles typically do; therefore, any discussion of its rhetoric and structure must investigate the question of genre broadly.

As an inheritor of the twin legacies of Greek medicine and Arabic belles lettres (*adab*), Ibn Buṭlān can hardly be said to have cut a unique figure by the standards of the fifth/eleventh century. Yet, despite his evident mastery of and reverence for these learned traditions, his unwillingness to conform narrowly to their conventions is a strong indication that *The Doctors' Dinner Party* can be read not as a simple rhetorical exercise or collection of bons mots, but as a farce, as displayed in his use of such techniques as wordplay, masking, and reversal. Indeed, *The Doctors' Dinner Party* is, foremost, an exhibition of the intricacy (*ʿawīṣ*, §0.1) of the Arabic language. A primary means of harnessing this variety is the use of lists in which medical jargon features often enough, as in the expositions of professional services (§1.6, §§1.8–9), surgical instruments (§2.12, §7.7), and materia medica (§9.11). At times, however, Ibn Buṭlān seems interested not so much in any particular medical issue as in demonstrating that the length of a given series is proportional to the specificity of the topic; here and there one finds directions for how thoroughly to chew food so as to ensure its proper digestion (§2.7), the physical and psychological benefits of wine (§3.2), the assortment of sounds one makes while drawing breath or exhaling (§10.17), and the symptoms of a mysterious illness (§11.7). No less striking are the catalogs of laurels for the city of Baghdad (§1.2) and Paradise (§2.8), various blessings and their concomitant obligations (§8.5), and examples of inappropriate verse to recite in front of various dignitaries (§11.9). Perhaps the most remarkable inventory in the work, however, is an enumeration of technical subjects in which a physician should be expert, juxtaposed with a practically scientific taxonomy of idle pastimes (§4.4; cf. §5.3). However, in his use of variegated linguistic registers Ibn Buṭlān eschews the neat prescriptions of categorization. Thus, on any given page the reader may encounter a number of vernacular phrases (§1.13, §9.1, §11.6), proverbs (§3.3, §4.4, §10.4), aphorisms attributed to ancient authorities (§1.12, §2.5, §10.9), a passage of rhymed and cadenced prose (*saj*ʿ, §1.10, §10.10), or examples of quoted and original poetry declaimed and sung to musical accompaniment (§3.4, §10.15). All this alongside an array of scatological or bawdy material related to homoeroticism (§3.5), marital infidelity (§9.10), nocturnal emission (§4.3), animal and human excrement (§10.8), flatulence (§6.3), and laxatives (§9.5). Even the graphical properties of the Arabic script provide the opportunity for ludic exploration, as epitomized in a number of sophisticated puns that hinge on the possibility of voweling a single consonantal outline in more than one way (e.g., the root *sh-m-m* (§9.4) and *khaṭṭ*/*khiṭṭ* (§10.18)).

As marvelous as these exercises in wordplay may be, it is important not to confuse their polyvocality with variety for its own sake, or to mistake itemization for manneristic flourish. These literary assemblages establish the conceptual and structural dimensions of the text, in which the depths of the most abstruse subjects can be sounded, and where the action is set against a sweepingly broad backdrop of cultural expression. The intricacy of the construction, however, only underscores the fact that this is a world in which not everything, or everyone, can be taken at face value.

The Doctors' Dinner Party was almost certainly influenced by the *Deipnosophists* (early third century AD), a "delightful feast of words [*logodeipnon*]" introduced by the "marvelous chief literary steward Athenaeus."[13] Book One of the *Deipnosophists* depicts a number of eminent guests, among whom sits Galen himself, listening to conversation about banquets and etiquette. It is a "feast of words" laid on for philosophers and writers, where food, though present, is never or hardly ever consumed, and it includes a discussion of avarice and party crashers. In *The Doctors' Dinner Party*, the host and his charlatan invitees are vultures, picking over a number of medical questions from another doctor's table—or so it seems, since if the questions are genuinely theirs, they provide no answers, in spite of their claim that even "hospital rats" know the answers.[14] A more tangible influence from Arabic literature is the trope of dinner guests being prevented from eating by the loquacity of a protagonist, normally the host, but sometimes a gate-crasher. And the presence of *maḍīrah*, the last savory dish at the dinner table, evokes the *Maqāmah Maḍīriyyah* of al-Hamādhānī, which is a grotesque banquet of words preventing consumption.[15] As Geert Jan van Gelder notes, "The main point of this *maqama* is the exposure of the boorish manners of some parvenus: its main technique is the motif of empty words instead of nourishing food."[16] If Ibn Buṭlān knew this *maqāmah*, he would likely also have read the *Maqāmah Ṭibbiyyah*, which satirizes flimflam fraudsters and parodies the literature of materia medica.[17]

The Doctors' Dinner Party is in some respects, as is so common in Arabic belletristic prose works, a chrestomathy of poetic quotations, drawn mainly from the classical period.[18] Most are highly attuned to the immediate context, such as when the oculist questions the youth and cites the lines of poetry borrowed from amatory verse about the deadly eye of the beloved. Abū Nuwās is a frequently quoted poet. This fact influences the way one interprets the narrative: once the four specialist invitees arrive, the narrative is structured, loosely yet noticeably, to echo one of the relatively extended narrative wine poems of Abū Nuwās, where initial sobriety leads to incapacitation and a loss of self-control. There is a detectable erotic subtext, stridently obnoxious though the players are. They assault the young guest with words, some of them a subterfuge for their physical attraction.

The first lines of poetry cited are verses from the amatory prelude of a poem, which are typically characterized by the theme of effacement. Here, the halcyon days of Baghdad have become effaced in the memories of both interlocutors. This notion of erasure resonates with *The Doctors' Dinner Party* as a whole, with its regret at the losses suffered by the medical profession and those who profess it. The negative images and metaphors that attach to the perceived state of medical practice are various: being a physician should be like having goods for sale, but in the "current climate" there is stagnation in the market; the health of the population, the absence of plague, is a curse. The narrative moves from equilibrium to disequilibrium, a transition mirrored in the state of the host himself.

The abuse of poetry, especially when good verse is placed in the mouths of scoundrels, is tangible in the poems of praise addressed to the Marwanid dedicatee, Naṣr al-Dawlah; these borrow lines from the praise poems of Abū Nuwās dedicated to al-Amīn (d. 197/813), the ill-starred caliph. Their evocation by the old fellow is therefore inauspicious, a major flaw in the poetic register of praise. Moreover, although Naṣr al-Dawlah is praised for restoring good health in his domain, this is the same health that is deplored by the doctor, who does not perceive the contradiction, as if trapped in each discrete moment of his individual utterances. For example, he praises the "intimacy of friends," yet has no real friends and wants to make Mayyafāriqin hateful to his young guest. The lack of hospitality extends through the banqueting scene, during which the old fellow—who is presented as pleasant, witty, and urbane when the young visitor first meets him in the marketplace—begins to show his true colors when he cautions against the consumption of food. At first the youth and his host debate coherently, each quoting ancient Greek sources as evidence; however, with words to the effect of "so you are determined to eat," the pique of the old fellow becomes tangible. He is aware of what he is doing, though unaware that his avarice is a vice, bringing a morbid set of surgical instruments into the room to warn the youth of the consequences of an unhealthy diet. He had first offered Indian medicine to his guest for his ailing stomach, but reneges on the offer at this second phase of the narrative, asking instead to be regaled with anecdotes about parasitic men. Having heard the youth's claim that he cannot drink, the old fellow now offers him appetizers, and when an old lyric song entertains the entourage, recalling a line of Abū Nuwās in which seductive kisses are held to be "the best appetizers," the youth responds that he can hardly be satisfied with the kisses of the present company. The old fellow takes umbrage and feels rejected by the young man.

The drinking party pursues its course with the absurd session of questions and answers, testing the youth; each session is preceded by a round of drinks from which the youth is consistently excluded. By the end, the old fellow is angrier still, and he derides the ignorance of people vis-à-vis medicine in a rambling tirade. *The Doctors' Dinner Party* ends with the old fellow stirring from his drunken stupor only to see that his delectable meal has been polished off by the youth and two others. He flies into a rage. This has been a travesty of a dinner invitation, compounded by anger and crude resentment: a long day's journey into night.

The medical question-and-answer format is another critical component of *The Doctors' Dinner Party*. This is the case not only because it structures the narrative, but because of its antecedents in medical literature, though it is important to note that in *The Doctors' Dinner Party* no answer is provided for any question. Ḥunayn ibn Isḥāq wrote one primer for medical students, titled *The Examination of the Physician* (*Miḥnat al-Ṭabīb*).[19] Unfortunately, it does not survive. Of the numerous treatises on the examination of physicians, some must have also been structured as questions and answers, such as al-Sulamī's (fl. early seventh/thirteenth c.) *The Experts' Examination of All Physicians*, "which contain extremely complicated and longwinded answers to questions which the students could hardly have been expected to answer."[20] As a parody of the genre, *The Doctors' Dinner Party* illustrates how common this fraudulent practice was perceived to be.

The Doctors' Dinner Party likewise includes many words of counsel: the old fellow is full of galling aphorisms. Like the verses of poetry that are quoted, they often resonate with the text in ironic and contrary ways. The young guest is advised by the old fellow that, in the military metaphor of medicine, a physician needs to know his enemy. This is as transparent in its irony as the advice, coming from an irascible counselor, to "let your reason overcome your passion." When the youth is counseled with an image of a tailor, to the effect of "measure twice, cut once," we can be sure in retrospect that this is a synecdoche for the entire narrative. The old fellow himself is anything but measured in this carefully calibrated text.

Similar to Ibn Buṭlān's strictly medical works, *The Doctors' Dinner Party* enjoyed demonstrable popularity among a geographically and confessionally diverse readership.[21] The evidence of its subsequent literary impact is scattered across a wide range of sources, including commentaries on the text, imitative works, quotations in anthologies, and biobibliographical sources. Indeed, the influence of *The Doctors' Dinner Party* was felt immediately by Ibn Buṭlān's contemporaries, as in a commentary on the questions posed by the shaykh and the other doctors by Ibn al-Athradī (d. between 472/1080 and 507/1113–14), like Ibn Buṭlān a student of Ibn al-Ṭayyib. From the next generation, the Damascene physician Muwaffaq al-Dīn Ibn Muṭrān (d. 587/1191) expressed his admiration for the literary merits of the work by penning an homage, known to Ibn Abī Uṣaybiʿah (d. 668/1269–70) simply as *A Composition, in the Style of "The Doctors' Dinner Party"* (*Kitāb ʿalā madhhab Daʿwat al-aṭibbāʾ*).[22] Concurrently, the work received a warm reception on the far western shores of the Mediterranean: Ibn Bassām al-Shantarīnī (d. 542/1147–48) quotes from it several times in *The Repository of the Virtues of the Inhabitants of the Iberian Peninsula* (*al-Dhakhīrah fī maḥāsin ahl al-Jazīrah*), and Ibn Zabārah (d. ca. 596/1200) appears to have used it as a model for his Hebrew-language "proto-novel" entitled *The Book of Delights* (*Sefer Shaʿashūʿīm*).[23] Around the same time, a copy of *The Doctors' Dinner Party* was made in Egypt, a fragment of which survives in the Taylor-Schechter Collection of the Cairo Genizah held at Cambridge University; several copies composed in Judeo-Arabic also survive.[24] Ibn Khallikān (d. 681/1282) and Ibn Abī Uṣaybiʿah each refer to a personal copy of *Daʿwat al-aṭibbaʾ*, and it is during their lifetimes that the extant textual tradition of this work comes into fuller view, as detailed in the table in the next section.[25]

*

Ibn Buṭlān's impressive work of fiction is far from being one-dimensional: it is not simply the encounter between an aged, bitter, and miserly doctor and a young would-be physician who turns out to be a charlatan. The work is full of allusions; it is an alloy of different generic influences, all written up in rich language, drawing on the Arabic belletristic tradition of *adab*, on poetry, and, hilariously, on the literature of medical deontology—questions and answers for physicians. A milestone in the *adab* tradition, this work masterfully unites a variety of cross-cultural inspirations. Given the author's enormous erudition and disputatious nature, the subject of *The Doctors' Dinner Party* could have been serious, but ends up being a multifaceted parody, or satire, or farce, or all of these, made all the more successful by the low moral fiber of its characters matched against astonishing sophistication in its psychology, imagery, and rich locution: a roman à clef, a novella, a drama, a skit, all flowing between registers of language and tone.

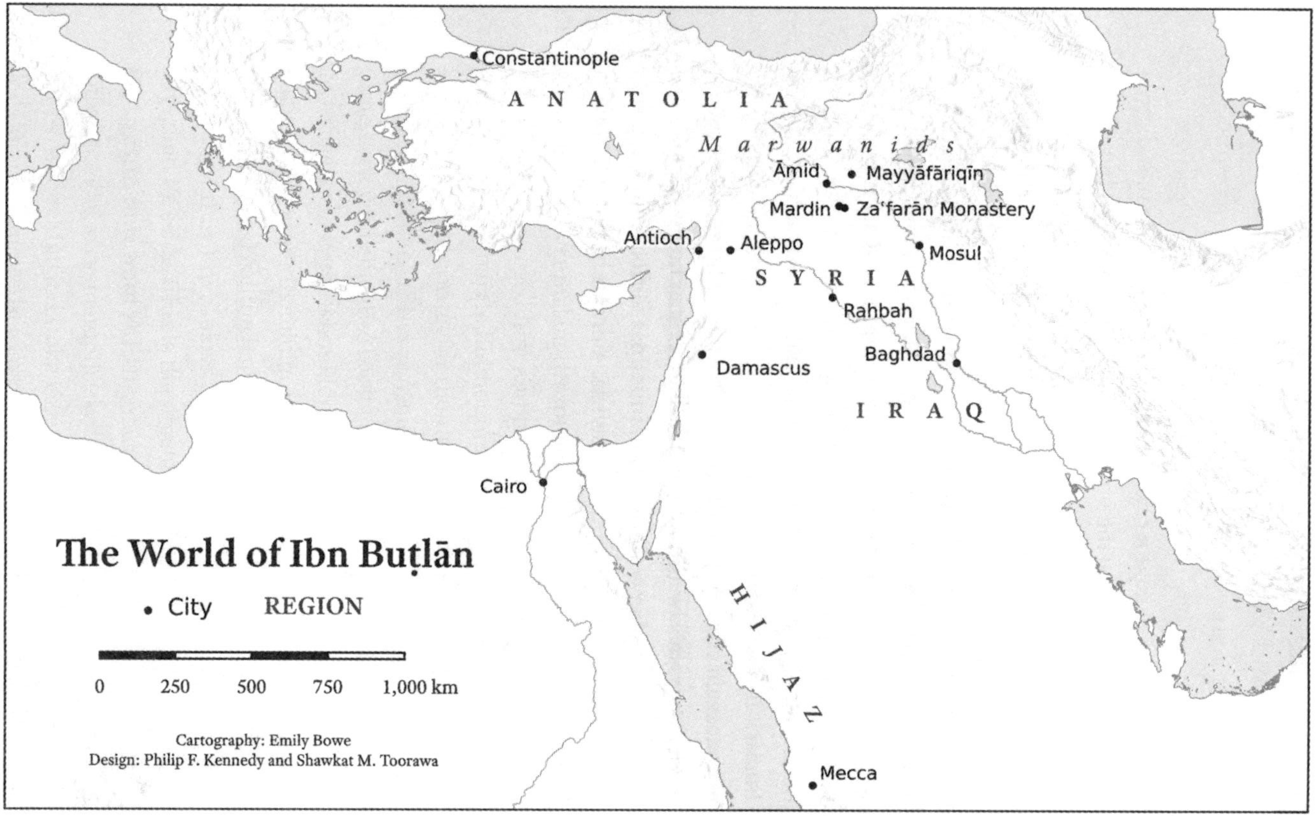

The World of Ibn Buṭlān
City
REGION
0
250
500
750
1,000 km
Cartography: Emily Bowe
Design: Philip F. Kennedy and Shawkat M. Toorawa
Constantinople
ANATOLIA
Marwanids
Āmid
Mayyāfāriqīn
Mardin
Zaʿfarān Monastery
Antioch
Aleppo
Mosul
SYRIA
Rahbah
Baghdad
Damascus
IRAQ
Cairo
HIJAZ
Mecca

Note on the Translation

Translation and medieval Islamic medicine go hand in hand. The Galenic humoral tradition was conveyed into Arabic culture by means of a concerted translation movement. This huge enterprise began in the early third/ninth century and was more or less complete by the end of the fourth/tenth century. A principal protagonist of the movement was the Nestorian Christian Ḥunayn ibn Isḥāq (d. 260/873). Writing several centuries later, the historian al-Ṣafadī (d. 764/1363) described Ḥunayn's translation technique as follows:

> The translators use two methods of translation. One of them is that of Yuḥannā ibn al-Biṭrīq [. . .] and others. According to this method, the translator studies each individual Greek word and its meaning, chooses an Arabic word of corresponding meaning, and uses it. Then he turns to the next word and proceeds in the same manner until in the end he has rendered into Arabic the text he wishes to translate. This method is bad [. . .].
>
> The second method is that of Ḥunayn ibn Isḥāq, al-Jawharī, and others. Here, the translator considers a whole sentence, ascertains its full meaning, and then expresses it in Arabic with a sentence identical in meaning, without concern for the correspondence of individual words. This method is superior; hence, there is no need to improve on the works of Ḥunayn ibn Isḥāq.[26]

As Savage-Smith and Pormann note, “These two methods are sometimes called *verbum de verbo* (word for word) and *sensum de sensu* (meaning for meaning) after a well-known expression by Cicero, the famous Roman statesman, orator, and philosopher (d. 43 BC).”[27]

If the Library of Arabic Literature endeavors to produce English translations of sometimes difficult premodern Arabic works for a broad anglophone readership, we owe it to ourselves not to render Arabic texts in an English riddled with transliterated Arabic terms. They are estranging and defamiliarizing, and stand in the way of creating an affinity with the text. The LAL is intent on producing translations in the spirit of the method championed by Ḥunayn.

However much one might strive for the streamlined style of Ḥunayn, the first drafts of a translation typically produce more *verbum de verbo* than *sensum de senso*. This is why it is important to rehearse and revise one’s translation with the help of other readers who need only concern themselves with how the English reads. This does not release the translator from the obligation of knowing the meaning of words, from understanding the grammar and the syntax of every line of the Arabic, or from admitting an aporia of certain comprehension. But it does, with the help of colleagues, promise greater hope that the work will be accessible to a wider audience.

We have accordingly invoked the help of more objective eyes that have not been caught in the gravitational pull of the Arabic. Such help has allowed our translation to scrub out infelicities and replace them with more convincingly modern and lucid versions of what the author was saying and—just as significantly—to attempt to approximate the tone and register in which he was saying it. Below are illustrative translations of poetry and of prose:

First pass:

I walked and wandered through its alleyways,
as distraught as a Qur’an in the home of a *zindīq*

Final rendering:

> I wandered its alleyways, distraught,
> like a Qur'an in a heathen's home (§1.4)

First pass:
They would teach them that which their natures move toward and their souls inclined toward and their hearts felt at ease with

Final rendering:
They would teach them whatever their hearts and souls naturally desired (§7.2)

Paradoxically, the modern register allows one to more easily travel back in time than would some archaic English language, allowing us for a few hours to inhabit without discomfort the world of a premodern text.

Notes to the Introduction

1 Conrad, "Ibn Butlān in *Bilād al-Shām*," 134n15.

2 On him, see Faultless, "Ibn al-Ṭayyib."

3 See Conrad, "Ibn Butlān in *Bilād al-Shām*," 136–37.

4 Conrad, "Ibn Butlān in *Bilād al-Shām*," 139.

5 A partial edition and translation can be found in Graf, "Die Eucharistielehre des Nestorianers Al-Muḫṭār ibn Buṭlan."

6 For further references to Ibn Buṭlān's contributions to Byzantine religious life, see Oltean, "From Baghdad to Antioch and Constantinople." For his influence on subsequent Byzantine medicine, see Pietrobelli and Cronier, "Arabic Galenism from Antioch to Byzantium: Ibn Buṭlān and Symeon Seth."

7 An excellent introduction to the subject is Savage-Smith and Pormann, *Medieval Islamic Medicine*. A helpful one-page summary of the humoral system of Galen can be found in al-Sulamī, *Questions and Answers for Physicians*, 15–16.

8 See Goitein, "The Medical Profession."

9 See *EI2*, "Ṭibb."

10 See Ibn al-Muqaffaʿ, *Kalīlah and Dimnah*, 23. Ibn Buṭlān repeats the same essential notion in the preamble to another work, *The Battle of the Doctors* (*Waqʿat al-aṭibbāʾ*), likely written after *The Doctors' Dinner Party* and on the heels of his run-in with Ibn Riḍwān.

11 As in a roman à clef, Ibn Butlān writes in his pious postscript that he uses pseudonyms for real people.

12 One autobiographical element is the vitriolic satire, which may reflect the vitriol Ibn Buṭlān experienced in his own life.

13 Athenaeus, *The Learned Banqueters*, 1:10.

14 For a comparative approach to the literary banquet, see Selove, *The Ḥikāyat Abī al-Qāsim*, 104–5.

15 For more on the *Maqāmah Maḍīriyyah*, see van Gelder, *God's Banquet: Food in Classical Arabic Literature*, 49–51; and Beaumont, "A Mighty and Never Ending Affair."

16 Van Gelder, *God's Banquet: Food in Classical Arabic Literature*, 50.

17 Recently discovered, this is clearly a pastiche of medical literature penned by al-Hamadhānī. See Orfali and Pomerantz, "A Lost Maqāma of Badīʿ al-Zamān al-Hamadhanī."

18 See the Index of Verses.

19 See Pormann, "The Physician and the Other: Images of the Charlatan in Medieval Islam," 210.

20 Savage-Smith and Pormann, *Medieval Islamic Medicine*, 86. See also al-Sulamī, *Questions and Answers for Physicians*.

21 Compared with the other works that enjoyed broad appeal, discussed in Marzolph, "The Migration of Didactic Narratives across Religious Boundaries."

22 Ibn Abī ʿUṣaybiʿah, *ʿUyūn al-anbāʾ fī ṭabaqāt al-aṭibbāʾ*, 15.23.5.6; cf. Ibn Buṭlān, *Daʿwat al-aṭibbāʾ*, ed. ʿUmar, 26n3.

23 For the characterization of the *Sefer Shaʿashūʿīm* as a "proto-novel," see Kozodoy, "The Physicians of Medieval Iberia (1100–1500)," 126.

24 For the date of the Genizah fragment, see Baker, "A Note on an Arabic Fragment of Ibn Buṭlān's 'The Physicians' Dinner Party' from the Cairo Geniza," 208. For examples of *Daʿwat al-aṭibbāʾ* copied in Hebrew script, see Fenton, *Ršiymat kitbey-yad bʿarbiyt-yhwdiyt bLeniyngrad*, 73, 113; and Szilágyi, "Christian Books in Jewish Libraries," 123n63.

25 E.g., Ibn Khallikān, *Wafayāt al-aʿyān wa-anbāʾ abnāʾ al-zamān*, 1:205; and Ibn Abī Uṣaybiʿah, *ʿUyūn*, 10.38.3, 10.38.5, 10.38.6.10 (s.v. "Ibn Buṭlān"); 10.54.1. (s.v. "Zāhid al-ʿUlamāʾ").

26 Savage-Smith and Pormann, *Medieval Islamic Medicine*, 27.

27 Savage-Smith and Pormann, *Medieval Islamic Medicine*, 27.

The Doctors' Dinner Party

The *Doctors' Dinner Party* is like *Kalīlah and Dimnah*. It includes humorous elements that lighten its serious parts, and fabrications that nevertheless convey the truth of the matter. This epistle, composed by Abū l-Ḥasan al-Mukhtār ibn al-Ḥasan ibn ʿAbdūn ibn Buṭlān for the emir Naṣr al-Dawlah Abū Naṣr Aḥmad ibn Marwān,[1] comprises the aphorisms of the Ancients, discourses of eloquent scholars, and well-chosen anecdotes about philosophers.[2] In this book, the scholar is wont to find what corresponds to his way of thinking and a student is apt to be led by what is conveyed in a straightforward way to an understanding of matters that are inherently abstruse; thus, if handled carefully and read attentively, this book will reveal the merit of skilled physicians and the impotence of the quacks in this profession. 0.1

It is divided into twelve parts.

Part the First—The "Opening Chapter"[3] of the book, in praise of Baghdad and denigration of Mayyāfāriqīn for its stagnation.[4] 0.2

Part the Second—Concerning the offering of a meal, and the presentation of decisive arguments against eating the foods provided.

Part the Third—A description of the symposium and its pleasures, and a conversation among the doctors present.

Part the Fourth—In which the Physiologist probes the extent of the guest's competence, thereby exposing his ignorance.

Part the Fifth—The ignorance of the guest revealed by the questions of the Oculist.

Part the Sixth—In which the Surgeon considers the guest's knowledge of anatomy and physiology.

Part the Seventh—The examination of the Phlebotomist on the requisite knowledge of the physiology of venesection.

Part the Eighth—The examination of the Apothecary on the guest's knowledge of remedies and medicines.

Part the Ninth—Concerning slanderous doctors who are scornful of the sick.

Part the Tenth—A defense of the devoted doctor and a denigration of the one who displaced him.

Part the Eleventh—The public's denigration of the medical profession and the riposte.

Part the Twelfth—The conclusion of the book and and a return visit rebuffed.

0.3 We ask God to grant us success in achieving correct exposition and eloquent phraseology so that what we produce may please God, Who prompted us to compose and assemble its disparate parts: He is the Generous Giver, the Close and Responsive.

Part the First: The "Opening Chapter" of the Book, in Praise of Baghdad and Denigration of Mayyāfāriqīn for Its Stagnation

I cite one of our sources: When I arrived in Mayyāfāriqīn, I inquired about the physicians practicing there. I was directed to a bench at the perfumers' market where an old fellow in his seventies was seated. He had fine, sharp features and was good humored and witty. He was courteous in argument and dispute, and stood out among his peers, clinging, as it were, to the coattails of good breeding. He was also skilled in the practice of medicine. I therefore approached and greeted him. He returned my greeting, made a space for me to sit, and received me with cordiality and respect. 1.1

"Who are you?" he asked. 1.2

"I'm a stranger tossed upon this canton by Fate," I replied.

"And what's your profession?" he continued.

"A doctor . . . ," I said.

"The most worthwhile and profitable profession! A medical practitioner is tantamount to a merchant with goods for sale! Where have you come from?"

"From Baghdad," I replied.

"Baghdad—the navel of the world," he declared, "the apex of the earth! The court of refinement, the trove of virtue. It is the abode of peace and the pinnacle of Islam, blessed by the presence of the caliph." He then recited:

"I love to stop at my old haunts,
dragging my hem on the ground.

1.3 "I traveled there for my studies. Those were halcyon days, each like a feast day or a Friday.[5] Its dust, in those days, was like antimony for your eyes, its pebbles like pearls around your neck. Scholars sold their wares in the markets according to the season, like all other goods. There I met the likes of Ibn Khammār and Ibn ʿAbdān, as well as Naẓīf ibn Yumn al-Qass, Ibn Baks, and Abū l-Wafāʾ the geometer."

I asked him why he left Baghdad and whether he had simply grown bored of the place. In answer, he recited a verse:

"I knew both banks of that city—
it was not rancor that pressed me to leave!"

"How," I asked, "could you bear to leave those great men when they were your ultimate goal?"

"I swear, when I came to this region none of those men were left," he replied.

"Is that all?" I asked.

And he recited:

"The years and all their folk too have vanished—
as if they were nothing more than dreams.

1.4 "It still grieves me that Fate dimmed those brilliant stars. Knowledge and science both died with them. But even had they lived until today, they would still die before their time: nowadays, good students willing to commit to their studies are rare, and we sell our books to merchants, goldsmiths, and salt sellers for all our basic needs and provisions. The profession has been eradicated, its fire has dimmed and gone out; those who try their hand at it are in it to make money, not to cure people. They say that bodies are healed with medicine wisely dispensed but that money makes doctors sick. If the physician brings sickness upon himself, how then can he cure others?

"Is there hope the invalid can be cured
when it's the doctor who afflicted him?"

He then asked me, "Why did you not stay in Baghdad?"

I answered:

"The rich stay in their homes
while men in search of food are cast far and wide."

And I added, "Don't you know these lines:

"Baghdad is good to the wealthy,
but the penniless know only anxiety and oppression.
I wandered its alleyways, distraught,
like a Qur'an in a heathen's home."

"Too true!" he said. "Now, why have you have come to these parts?" 1.5

"I am heading to the Zaʿfarān Monastery and intend to practice medicine there if I find the place agreeable."

He was upset when he learned of my intentions and said, "God forbid! This place has a better reputation than it deserves! The efforts you expended in coming here have been in vain. If you'll permit the expression, 'Your flint will not spark.' I only wish I were like you and could flee this place without constraint. I detest it here now. When I first started living here, with few exceptions, I met only honorable folk. When they were all together, they were like precious jewels, and when they dispersed, they were like scattered pearls:

"Any you encountered, you would say was noble,
each a star guiding the traveler by night."

"What has become of them?" I asked.

And he replied, "They've all died, sons and servants too. They used up all my medical opinions and exhausted my nights as I treated them, until God ordained their deaths. May He pour rain upon their graves—while they lived, they sheltered me from the vicissitudes 1.6

of time! Their charity and largesse ensured I was never without a young girl to wean, a young boy to circumcise, someone to bleed for the first time, or a sick man to escort to the baths—not to mention the presents they gave me on feast days, such as Nowruz, and other things patients usually bring to the consulting room as token gifts. Whenever a patient of mine died, two others would fall ill in his place. I was sitting pretty, a proud man who excited wonder, like Qirwāsh ibn al-Muqallad or the ruler of Mayyāfāriqīn. Nowadays, when we're stretched so thin, we bleed two veins for a single penny. I'd be finished if I didn't have some clients left who have seasonal dropsy!

1.7 "The funny thing in all this is that we used to have plenty of patients in the autumn. And every five years we'd have a deadly plague. But since the Marwanids have been in power our profession has no purchase and our 'goods' go to waste. Everyone is now healthy in these parts, plague is on the retreat, and dropsy is all but gone. Before, it was only rarely that we were free of throat infections. Autumn ailments no longer afflict anyone—they used to be a sure thing. Now we see a sick person only once in a while, funeral processions are few and far between, and lengthy stretches separate the times we hear wailing for the dead. It's almost as if the accession of this ruler has rendered all bodies immune from disease, and put an end to all aching limbs. You might say that people have taken sanctuary with the Marwanids against fate. Everyone now sings these lines by Abū Nuwās:

"I'm tied to Muḥammad by the ropes of friendship,
safe with him from the blows of Fate;
Nestled in his wing, I take shelter.
I see my fate but it cannot see me:
Asked my name, it cannot answer,
nor tell where I live.

1.8 "How content he is with himself and his people, but how heavily he treads on our welfare since he has taken command of this region.

No one takes us into consideration: everyone ignores us because we are no longer needed, even though back in the day in this town the physician was considered more radiant than the brightest star in the sky.[6] The gravediggers and coffin bearers have put great distance between themselves and here. They've all dispersed to the outlying villages and garrisons. Most of them have found bit work in agriculture, raising crops or yoking oxen to plow the fields, or else gathering gypsum from the hilltops for construction in town. Every now and again I meet one of them who is unemployed and try to console him, even as he imagines the good old days will return:

"May the Fates[7] return a people
to their former glorious times.

"My dear sir, what else can I tell you about those bygone days? 1.9
Corpses were carried in procession to the graveyard bedecked in silk shrouds, looking like gardens in bloom. One day during the plague, we counted two hundred corpses being carried through the city gate toward the cemetery. Those were just my own patients, not counting those of my colleague next to me here. Every day you would see fifty mules—belonging to soldiers, chancery officials, and merchants' couriers—tied up outside my door. That year I became vainer than ʿUmārah ibn Ḥamzah and mightier than ʿAmr ibn Maʿdīkarib. But who among us now can restore that state of affairs?

"I have tasted pain the likes of which
Abū l-Ḥusayn the dentist could not remove from my molars!

"Dear brother, where were you when no one in this town was 1.10
sane or could do without treatment and medication? The funeral processions wended their way through town like wedding parties, arriving at the gravesites like flowers in bloom, while mourning voices sang as if accompanied by the din of flutes and tambourines. When the services of corpse washers could only be obtained through sweet talk, and physicians would queue outside their stalls ready with their laden mules? Today, in truth, these same folk

seek menial employment, cleaning their jars and phials, choosing between this or that party while musicians play melodies on the oud and sing these lines by Abū Nuwās:

> "We are bound to the emir by ropes
> that protect us from the storms of Fate!

1.11 "So, my dear sir, what are you doing in this town? I can spend a month and a day here without a single solicitation for treatment, without a single funeral procession passing by, and if ever God does show me clemency and sends me a sick man, it is as the saying goes: 'The juice isn't worth the squeeze!' My friend, I've had my fill of this town—its people bore me! It's like the old expression: 'When water stagnates it begins to stink, and the longer it lingers the more nauseating it becomes.' I have often told myself I should leave this place. But then I say to myself, Where will I go? Whom should I visit? Most of my life is behind me—where should I wander as a stranger? Well, every day has its tomorrow. The only thing keeping me here is the intimacy of friends, even though time only propels us backward as it moves forward!"

Of course, his only intention in saying all this was to make me hate the idea of staying there.

1.12 He then asked me, "Tell me now, what have you come to do at the Zaʿfarān Monastery?"

And I answered, "Sir, I have heard the saying of Galen that to compare our medicine with temple medicine is like comparing it with the quack medicine of highwaymen pretending to be doctors. I am a man with a weak stomach and little appetite. There is no cure I haven't tried; I was told there is a great monk in this monastery, one of those who have seen the world for what it is and set it aside: I am on my way to meet him and to ask for his blessing."

The old fellow laughed and said, "You're acting just like the man who had cataracts in both eyes. He met a friend who said, 'I see you put up with sore eyes for a long time—what are you treating them with?' 'By appealing to my mother in prayer,' he said, to which the friend responded, 'She will answer your prayers more quickly if you add a little sarcocolla balsam to your eyes!' Now, a *zāmaharān*[8] electuary would be more effective in strengthening your stomach and improving your appetite than having recourse to this monk. This is an Indian medicine I have myself prepared. I'll set some aside for you, enough for you to feel better. Now, tell me, how is your digestion? And how much are you eating these days?"

"My appetite is very poor," I replied, "and I eat only morsels of food."

Content with my answer about my ailing stomach and reduced 1.13
appetite, he said, "Come home with me, I beg you! We'll share some food and chat. I enjoy your company since you are not from these parts and our conversation will remain private. I rarely feel good about people—I'm like the flash of a mirage with companions and friends!

> "Your enemy gets help from your friend,
> so keep the company of few.
> Most ailments one encounters
> stem from food and drink!"

I resisted his invitation and assured him that I had already eaten. But he insisted, and so I accompanied him to his house.

Part the Second: Concerning the Offering of a Meal, and the Presentation of Decisive Arguments against Eating the Foods Provided

We sat talking for a while, and then a young servant boy appeared with a tray covered with a cloth on which he placed bread and vinegar. Once he had set it down before us, the old fellow declaimed: 2.1

"Generosity is not heaping hospitality on your guest.
It is the gracious face of the host that is generous!
I make my guest laugh even before he dismounts.
He feels abundance in my presence no matter how barren the place.

"My friend," he continued, "you must excuse me! As the saying goes:

"When visited unannounced, offer what you have at hand.
When you throw a party, spare no expense.

"But the days have been long and have had their effect!"

He then took a loaf of bread and said, "God rest my old lady's soul! She used to take every trouble to bake good bread and taught this young man to do the same. Eat! The wheat has been washed, the dough has been raised, and it is not too salty. It is seasoned at its base with condiment from the *khalanj* tree; it has a pinkish crust, is easy to chew, is quickly digested, and sits well in the stomach." He then reached for a bunch of chicory and said, 2.2

"Good sir, the best chicory has fine and tender fibers; it is quicker than all other kinds of chicory in nourishing the liver and is the best in clearing intestinal blockages; its juice is often served with rhubarb. See, my dear sir, how broad and green are its leaves. Taste how sweet, luscious, and fresh it is, especially when accompanied by this sharp vinegar. See! It is the only thing I can rely on to cure my jaundice. God curse the servant boy! His coarseness knows no bounds. A few days ago he served me some vinegar that had been too lightly mixed. I blithely took some of it, and no sooner did it touch my tongue than it rushed to my throat and head. My nose bled immediately, tears poured from my eyes, and I began to cough. I was in discomfort for several days. Have some," he continued, "but be careful!"

2.3 When I made to eat, he said, "Aren't you planning on following an ailing man's diet?"

"Perhaps on an appropriate day," I replied.[9]

And he retorted, "Worse than guilt is despair of God's mercy! More grievous than sin is delaying repentance; more insidious than illness is postponing a healthy diet. Intervening too late is of no use to the one in need, and a physician who assails his patient is a harbinger of the angel of death. When a sick man aggravates his condition by eating, he is like a silkworm: the more he persists in his ways, the more of his life he leaves behind."

I replied that I hated these sorts of diet, and he said, "Heavens! A healthy diet is difficult, to be sure, but the most rewarding actions are those hateful to the soul. Pythagoras said that controlling one's stomach brings one's organs and body parts closer to a healthy equilibrium. Since you have mastered medical practice, I didn't think you would need any such advice: it is as unseemly for a physician to be thought confused as for a jurist to be dissolute. Choose God's path and stick to this diet with determination. Look to your food and the form it takes as soon as tomorrow. How astute was Socrates when he passed by a street sweeper cleaning food scraps from his broom: 'You people of Athens, this is what you lock behind your doors and appoint guards to protect. You let your appetites rule your minds when preparing your food, but today you shun it in disgust just as this street sweeper does.'" He then said, "Prepare to behave according to what I've said, for this advice is given in good faith—it is an admonition girdled with wisdom."

When I began to eat, he grabbed my hand and said, "Listen to what I have to say before you eat; it will cure what ails you and restore your health. The first step in treating one's ailments is to purse one's lips and discipline one's hands to go easy on the food. A sick man should handle his sickness by relying on his mind, not on appetites born of desire and ignorance. The mind seeks the most beneficial kind of nourishment, whereas desire seeks the most appetizing and delicious. Rarely do natural benefit and palatability come together in a single item. Food seldom has natural benefit, and medicine is just as seldom as tasty. Beware, good sir, of taking pleasure in the tastiness of food and finding loathsome the bitterness of medicine. 2.4

"Bitterness is sweet when it benefits
  and sweetness bitter when it harms,[10]
So take something bitter that might benefit you
  and shun sweets that will harm!

"And beware of fleeting delights—they cause harm in the long term, especially since you're ill and bloated with food."

"Sir, it's digested and I'm ravenous," I said, and he responded with, "A false pang! This craving is nothing but a mirage," and began to recite:

"There are specific times for digestion;
  everything has its balance and limits.
Do not be hasty in the treatment you seek—
  the disease must progress before you feel better."

"What do you think of measuring out time for eating and digestion?"[11] I asked. 2.5

He said, "Sound opinion dictates abstention: Disease only increases when you pile food upon food. This is what kills the beasts in the wild. When indigestion lingers it kills, just as it weakens a body that isn't functioning properly. Hippocrates says, 'Do not be deceived by ill timing, such as when a patient grows hungry before he has properly convalesced.'"

"Sir," I answered, "surely you also know that the Ancients say that food is to the ailing person like provisions to the traveler—and illness is like a journey. That is why a physician shouldn't neglect the strength that food provides lest it dissipate entirely before the end of an illness."

He responded, "But you know that Hippocrates said that ailing bodies are harmed by excessive food?"

"You're right," I answered, "but the Ancients also say that one should be lenient with the patient with respect to some of his appetites. There is greater benefit from unhealthy food with an appetite than vice versa."

"This is true," said the shaykh, "but the Ancients also mention that bodies filled with surplus food turn the alimentary benefits into natural waste."

I said, "They also said you should avoid treating illness with medicine when you can make do with nutritious food."

The shaykh answered, "Remember that your stomach is indisposed and your gut not cleansed, so I can't be sure you won't succumb to terrible sickness if you touch food."

"My good sir," I answered, "I will eat and seek God Almighty's help."

"All strength and power come from God!" he exclaimed. "If your time is up, the cause will be in your stomach!"

2.6 I ignored him and made to eat, at which he exclaimed, "So you're eating, then? Go easy! Know—may God cure you—that knowledge is to the mind like food to the body. Poor sustenance kills the body, weakens both strength and spirit, and will make you the lowest of the low. The spirit is purified with true knowledge and takes the body with it to the loftiest heights, where the spiritual reside; to the place of might and greatness, where the sources of splendor and salvation abide. Hippocrates says, 'It is not with bread alone that man is revived but with sound words'; Socrates says, 'If you have designs to eat, do not eat merely for the sake of eating'; and Plato says, 'I eat to live, I do not live to eat.' So beware of throwing yourself upon this food. Slow down: be like the nimble tailor who measures his thread a thousand times before cutting in haste. No good comes from hurrying! Heed the words of the old poet:

> "To succeed, take your time.
> Failure is the handmaid of haste!"

"Well," I answered, "why shouldn't I take heed rather of the poet who said:

> "Being sluggish, the dawdlers lost their eminence.
> It would have been sensible for them to hurry."

"Well then," he said, "if you're determined to eat, at least take small morsels. Nibble them into fine pieces with your incisors and canines, and chew them well with your molars. Turn them about with your tongue and swallow only what you have crushed into a paste, then continue chewing and grinding with your molars. Have vegetables and herbs before you have stew, and avoid all condiments." He then recited: 2.7

> "Your soul will fortify your appetite if you let it,
> but it will be satisfied if you stand firm and consume in moderation.

"Beware of meat," he continued, "for Hippocrates says, 'Do not let your stomachs become graveyards for animals.'[12] And Galen says, 'The most ignorant people are those who fill their stomachs with whatever they find.' In the fight against jaundice, rely on acids; against phlegm, on salty foods; and against melancholy, on fatty soups. You should know that jaundice is like a young lad who is content with a bauble but angered by a word of reproof, that melancholy is like a bull led by a woman and child but uncontrollable when angry, and that phlegm is like a prowling lion that will kill unless killed first. Keep your phlegm in check as you do your servant. Subdue your bile as you do one who pins you down. Be at peace with your blood as you are with your friend. And fight melancholy as you would your enemy. Restrict the varieties of foods you eat—they upset the stomach and impede digestion. Do not eat what your teeth have a hard time chewing, which your stomach will then be unable to digest. My dear sir, divide what reaches your intestines into three parts: one part food, one part drink, and one part air. There's more to life than running back and forth to the latrine, so be mindful at mealtime; surely, you won't suddenly find spare room in your stomach after you've gorged yourself on food and finished physically and chemically digesting it. Do not drink too much cold water during the various courses of your meal. And make sure your reason overcomes your passions: Few have let their passions dominate them without being ruined. Few have run after women without causing scandal. Few have engaged in evil without perishing. Few have overeaten and drunk excessively without falling ill." He wouldn't stop raving and prattling on about this, and preventing me from eating.

2.8 He then set off on a lengthy speech that encompassed all mannner of idle talk; I ignored him and proceeded to eat, starting with the vinegar and greens. He did not order more food until he felt I was satisfied and was satiated by the vinegar and greens. He then told his servant boy, "Take this away and bring in the roast meat." The boy came back with an entire roasted lamb.

I reached for the shoulders, and the old fellow launched in, "Beware of those! Its undigested remains will sit heavy upon your heart." I reached for the lamb's throat, and he said, "Do not expose yourself to this, it will slow your digestion." I reached for the kidneys, and he said, "This is the organ where urine and blood settle." So I gestured toward the thighs, and he said, "These lie near the intestines and excrement." I asked permission to take the haunches, but he said, "My God, take care! It is unwholesome, and will kill your appetite and cause summer cholera." "What," I asked, "should

I go for then?" and he said, "The limbs' extremities—those are the tastiest part of the sheep, especially one newly weaned." So I made to take the extremity closest to me, and he said, "Are you taking the hind parts when the forelimbs are superior? And are you taking from the right side when the left side is better, since it is closer to the heart and the body's natural heat and farther from impurities and the sickening surfeits of the body's intake? Take what I give you and avoid all else, which can only harm you."

He gave me a piece from the trotters scant in meat and said, "Take this right-hand morsel, for the animal put its weight upon it while pasturing and trotting about. Come, my boy, take it." And he told his young servant, "Take this away. Let's elude his misfortune and ensure his safety. In satisfying one's appetites there are many paths to ruin and painful side effects. Often indulging in a single dish leads to being deprived of several others. He should eat foods that are wholesome for him and avoid those that can only harm his constitution. Bring in what you have." So the boy brought in *maḍīrah* stew. I began to eat and he said, "You should know, God help you!, that a person likes only those foods that agree with him and not those that are harmful to him. This is beef *maḍīrah*, which the Ancients forbade to those suffering from your ailment. They proscribed the mixing of beef and milk products just as they did the mixing of beef and fish. Heavens! It is the source of all joint pains—gout, facial palsy, colic, hemiplegia. God protect you from the harm this stew will cause you." Then he again told his servant, "Take the dish away from us. Removing it can only result in good. I can't after all guarantee that our guest, what with his passions and his appetite, will not fall foul of harmful ailments from the effects of this *maḍīrah*." 2.9

The dish was taken away and a milk rice pudding that had been cooked underneath the lamb was brought. I suspected that nothing else would be forthcoming after this, so I felt the need to satisfy my appetite with it. As I moved in to eat it, he perceived my intention. Anger showed clearly on his face, and he signaled to his servant to take the dish away. The boy assumed he was calling for dessert and 2.10

brought a bowl of *fālūdhaj*; it was pleasantly colored with food dye and was a decent-sized portion. His anger grew and the goblet was filled with the spatter of his tears. He said, "God protect us from the evil the fates have set upon us. Know, my good man, that the person who commands good is no happier than the person who obeys him, and the person who offers advice is no more deserving of counsel than the person he counsels. So heed my advice—sweet desserts ruin your teeth and cause pustules to form in the mouth and on the tongue, especially when followed by iced water. Al-Ma'mūn once complained about his ailing teeth to Jibrīl ibn Bukhtīshūʿ, who said to the caliph, 'Commander of the Faithful, abstain from iced water after eating ripe dates and sugary dishes.' 'Damn you, Jibrīl,' replied the caliph, 'it's precisely because of these two dishes that I need your medicine. What pleasure remains for the tongue if one must desist from iced water and sweets?' So he went against Jibrīl's advice, and we all know that his teeth suffered as a result.

2.11 "So I am asking you to put down that bowl. A wise man does not give precedence to his pleasure over his health. Now, tell me what you have decided."

And I said, "I've decided to eat and leave the outcome in God's hands."

"Do you think that by setting aside desserts you are abandoning your trust in God?" he asked. And he went on: "You should know that a physician is a mediator between God and the patient; the mediator partakes of both sides of this equation: from God's attributes he takes mercy and charity, and from the sick he takes entreaty and need. His goal is well-being and he is assiduous in offering good advice, as he aspires to attain what is wholesome for every human soul:

"When a soul feels anger toward the body
 he mediates between the two,
As if, with subtle thoughts,
 he intervenes between flesh and bones.

“Do not think badly of me, and do not attribute my words and deeds to stinginess. You need advice; it should not sit heavily upon you. God knows how often I crave delicious foods, preferring them to all else, but then I fear their noxious effect and forbid myself from indulging. Often, when I’m overcome by craving, I remind myself of the pain and discomfort they cause and call for my medical instruments to be placed before me.” He then said to his servant, “Take away the dessert! Bring what you have!” 2.12

I was certain it would be another silver bowl or some dish to round off the meal. But no! Instead, what I saw on the table was a tray with an array of instruments: pincers for extracting molars, hot irons for the spleen and head, forceps for applying and removing leeches, sharp arrowheads and needles for treating cataracts and conjunctivitis, syringes for colic, urinary catheters, hemorrhoid hooks, cone-shaped devices for clearing the nostrils, lead weights, saws for amputation, instruments for couching cataracts, scoops for cleansing the ears, cleaving irons, a probe for tumors, a scraper for scabies, a shoulder splint, bandages for supporting the hip, forceps for the uterus, a spindle for the sciatic nerve, plaster for the intestines, a lancet for pleurisy, drops for eye treatment, an ointment pot, and a scalpel receptacle.

As I contemplated this tray of instruments, I became anxious 2.13
about eating and imagined an awful end.

“Good sir,” he said, “man should thank God Almighty for his health and pray for it to last. Don’t all these instruments exist because of the effect on the body of eating and chewing?

> “So much refuse is ingested with food
>   it drives the soul from the body!
> God withholds His blessing from food
>   since souls are destroyed by the stomach.”

He then said to his servant, “Spare us all these foods and bring in the basin and some alkali salts.” We washed our hands, but he interrupted me while I was washing, took a cushion, reclined on it, and said, "Good sir, let's chat. It's the perfect time for it. Abū ʿAlī Naẓīf, God rest his soul, always used to say:

"I have grown weary of my desires;
even the best ones seem wretched,
Except for conversation,
which always promises novelty."

2.14 The old fellow began to limber up for conversation. He grew confident and gathered his energy, ready to craft precious words, and recited:

"Hold strong against the smug—I'll show them:
I do not cower before Fate's blows."

"Sir," I said, "since I am on a diet, I am keen to try that electuary you referred to before. Will you tell me when I can take it? How much will I need?"

"This isn't such a tough nut to crack," he replied. "You are more in need of something that will curb your appetite than something that will strengthen your stomach. Forget about it! And instead tell me some good stories you know."

"You mean stories about Bunān?" I said.

"What about in verse?"

I replied that I knew a poem about sponging and freeloading.

"Is it well known? Popular with people?"

So I recited:

"We visit you, not repaying your scorn in kind:
the generous man visits the one who stays away.
Longing makes a distant house seem close:
follow your yearning and no house will seem too far."

"What skill have you specialized in?" he asked.

"Cuisine," I replied.

"What medicine have you studied?"

"The treatment of convalescents," I replied.

"And what ailment has debilitated your stomach?" he asked.

"Having a canine appetite!" I said.

He then asked, "What made you leave Baghdad?"

"Inflation," I said, "and the cost of living—I suffered greatly there."

He grew angry, and sat upright from his reclining position and recited:

> "Fate has judged between people:
>   What is disastrous for some is a boon for others."

"Sir," I said to the old fellow, "if you despair of my cure, can I ask about another thing I suffer from?"

"Go ahead! I hope it is a worthwhile question," he replied.

"Why is it that I cannot drink wine and that it disagrees with my stomach on any and all occasions?" I asked.

He liked what he heard and said, "This is indeed a curious trait—that the stomach should be strong when it comes to eating but weak when it comes to drinking."

Part the Third: A Description of the Symposium and its Pleasures, and a Conversation among the Doctors Present

What I'd said made him happy and he laughed. Taking my words at face value, he asked his boy to bring in the wine. The boy brought in a tray with appetizers and wine, and then fetched the old fellow's goblet and rinsed it. The old fellow asked me to admire its beauty, saying, "This is loot from the emir's palace during the rebellion against the old regime.[13] I used to have an even more beautiful one, but I had to sell it when things got too difficult this winter." Then he recited: 3.1

> "Umm Malik, precious curios may come from the coffers
> of a man unwilling to give them up.

"Halcyon days are bound to return and make up for the loss, especially as this last winter of ours was windy and rainy, and this spring full of changes in the weather—I think, God willing, it will be a plague year."

He then filled his goblet and said, "This is a wine we've long cherished. Hippocrates observed that it settles one's thirst and relieves the pangs of hunger. It has ten benefits, five bodily and five spiritual. The bodily ones are: it helps digestion, is a diuretic, is good for the skin, freshens the breath, and augments the pleasure of orgasm. The spiritual ones are: it makes one happy, gives one hope, emboldens the heart, enhances one's mood, and keeps stinginess at bay." 3.2

3.3 He then took a swig and said to his boy, "Go to my student Abū Jābir the phlebotomist and invite him here; tell him to bring his oud. Then go and fetch my good friend Abū Ayyūb the oculist, and Abū Sālim the surgeon. As for Abū Mūsā the apothecary, tell him, 'Let me be your *soul* client today.'"

They were not long in arriving. We exchanged formal greetings and they asked who I was, so the old fellow told them about my circumstances. They then all began to complain about the hardships they suffered while trying to earn a living. They reminded each other of the parlous state of pharmacology. I saw before me people who took refuge in learning but were for the most part vulgar.

They were silent for a while and then began to discuss a serious issue. The old fellow said, "'Wine today, business tomorrow.'[14] Today we should neither lecture nor teach since constant devotion to science destroys the spirit. Galen said that the learned need to cease intellectual pursuit for a while in order not to debilitate the body, which is the instrument of all strength and action."

3.4 When his cup was refilled, he said to his student, Abū Jābir, "The Ancients say that the oud is built on four medical natures:[15] the lutist's plectrum is like the cupper's scalpel; the strings are like the body's veins; the lines on the face of the lute are like the nerves—so be careful not to pluck the strings clumsily and hit the soundboard. Now, keeping this in mind, sing us the verses by Abū Nuwās about our master, the doctor Jibrīl ibn Bukhtīshūʿ." Abū Jābir began to play, and sang:

"I asked my brother Abū ʿĪsā, the great and gifted Jibrīl:
'Wine delights me; what should I do?'
'Too much of it kills,' he said.
'Measure it out?' I asked.
And he answered with grace:
'Man has four humors,
So measure out four for four—
one portion for each humor.'"

He then launched into a new tune:[16]

"Take me away from these effaced traces
 as I stand over unfamiliar spring haunts.
Give me drink as I listen to the strum of the strings
 syncopated with the drone of the drums.
Then strike the strings gently,
 as Hippocrates would, feeling for a pulse."

They were in thrall, and all drank but me. When I despaired of receiving a cup, I began to eat the appetizers and asked, "Which, good sir, is the healthiest appetizer?" 3.5

"The caliph al-Mutawakkil asked Jibrīl the same question," he said, "and Jibrīl replied, 'The appetizer of Abū Nuwās, sire,' and al-Mutawakkil asked, 'And what is that?,' and he replied with a line of poetry:

"'I have looked everywhere for better,
 but wine is finer than water, and kisses more savory than canapés!'

"You're in the same position," the old fellow said.

"True," I replied, "but Jibrīl said this to al-Mutawakkil when there were twelve thousand women serving him in his palaces. Am I supposed to be satisfied instead with the likes of Abū Ayyūb the oculist and Abū Sālim the surgeon?"

This made him angry.

"Didn't you say you were a doctor?"

"Indeed I am," I replied.

"What's your specialty, then?"

"Physiology."

Part the Fourth: In Which the Physiologist Probes the Extent of the Guest's Competence, Thereby Exposing His Ignorance

He said, "Let me ask you a question." 4.1

"Go ahead."

He began to recite:

> "Deliver me, Lord, from anguish and sickness:
> from an ailing soul in need of cure
> And from my foibles, too—
> forgive them, for I cannot endure their cure."

He then came back to the point and said, "Let me ask you some questions."[17] 4.2

"Go ahead," I replied.

"Do not think," he began, "that I will ask you why the Ethiopians and Slavs, from different countries and of opposing natures, both eat warm dry foods, drink wine, and perfume themselves with musk and amber, whereas they ought to behave in opposite ways. I will not ask you about that, because this is a matter of general agreement. Mind you, the answer is not that the Ethiopians use such things as medicine and the Slavs consider them to be nourishment, lest you think it necessary to follow the practice of the Ethiopians during the summer and that of the Slavs during the winter. And I will not ask you about swine, which are the most well balanced of animals in terms of constitution. They should feed on the most balanced vegetation and yet they consume the vilest human waste—all this is written about and well known. What's more, I will not ask you why the Ancients divided phlegm into its tastes and why they considered vitreous and tasteless phlegm one of those tastes; and why they considered it cold whereas it is warmer than blood in the third stage of digestion. Nor will I ask you about parturition and whether or not it is natural when it involves three types of sickness—even as it is the source of all human nature.

4.3 "Rather, I will ask you this: A continent man might sleep and dream that he is urinating, though he is not in fact; he then wakens—the urine has forced him to waken and pass water."

"Yes," I acknowledged.

"And that same man may see in his dream that he is making love and ejaculate; he then wakes up and finds that he has spilled semen on his clothes."

"Yes," I said.

"So why is it," he asked, "that the urine is not evacuated despite its relative quantity and can wait till the man wakens, whereas the sperm is secreted in sleep and does not wait till he wakens, despite its relatively exiguous measure, when they are both emissions?"

"I do not know," I said.

And he retorted, "So the person who doesn't know about his own urine throws himself upon the appetizers!"

4.4 He then turned to the others and said, "It is true that he does not know because greed puts intelligence to flight. Heavens! If Hippocrates had eaten as he eats we would think the mental faculties dwell in the stomach."

Then he then addressed me ironically: "You were born under a propitious sign.[18] Yet if a doctor does not concern himself with medical matters; with the lives of the Ancients; with researching the opacities in the works of Hippocrates and in Galen's sixteen canonical books; with the solar and lunar cycles that influence the course of an illness; and with growth, and whether or not it stems from the limbs or the bodily organs; and with the pulse, when its single beat, or regular beats, is irregular—what then *does* concern him? Is he preoccupied with stories about effeminates and singers, with Ibn Surayj's pleasant melodies, with Maʿbad's songs, with the numerous pleasant stories about the elder Bidʿah, with the trilling voice of the sublime Surayrah or the rhythms of Muzāḥim the dancer? If he cannot be satisfied with the handbooks and manuals of prescribed medical practice, then which books does he look to? Pulp titles, filled with lovers' tales? With descriptions of comely figures, rosy cheeks, and alluring eyes, of batting eyelids, and pining and longing? With the pleasures of lovers' trysts and the pangs of their separation? And the woes Qays faced with Lubnā, Majnūn with Laylā, and Jamil with Buthaynah?"[19]

"Sir," I said, "I am not a physiologist."

"What are you, then?"

"An oculist!"

"That subject is Abū Ayyūb's bailiwick."

Part the Fifth: The Ignorance of the Guest Revealed by the Questions of the Oculist

The old fellow said to Abū Ayyūb, "Down this cup and ask your questions." 5.1

He took the cup, raised it, pondered over it intently, and said, "By God, as the poet said:

> "The glass is like a crystalline drop of water
> and the precious wine a fiery flame.

"By heaven, my friend, sing to us the verses of our teacher, Israel the Oculist."

And he broke into song:

> "They said his eye pains him—
> the deadly mix of water has caused its lesion,
> Its redness tainted by the blood of a murdered victim,
> the blood on his spear tip an extraordinary witness."

Then he warbled another song:

> "His eyes are sick without sickness or cause,
> embellished with kohl, with no kohl applied.
> His beauty groaned at his foul and ugly deeds
> and embarrassment tinged his cheeks red."

5.2 They all took another drink without me; then Abū Ayyūb asked me, "If a peddler applied a medical balm to your donkey's eye without your knowledge and blinded the beast, claiming it was suffering from an eye condition in order to wager that applying another ointment would cure its sight, well, do you know which medication covers the tunics of the eye, blocking its humors and thus impeding vision, and which other medication when applied immediately removes the obstruction?"

"No," I replied.

5.3 Our host weighed in: "O poverty of in*sight*! Did you think he was interrogating you about when cataracts constitute the cause of disease and when they are the disease itself? Or about Galen—namely, why was he critical of small eyes while praising the qualities of small pupils? God forgive you! How did you misspend your youth, dear sir? I'll wager you spent the time obsessed with drinking sessions, morning and night, keeping the company of like-minded friends, mesmerized by singing girls, learning the various names of wine and how an ensemble compensates for the lack of a percussionist by substituting an oboist, frequenting literary salons, seeking out perfect fragrances, squeezing etrogs, consuming the juice of mandrake plants, arranging lute strings, and tuning instruments according to a well-tempered system: the first string for both heavy and light modes, and the other strings in *ramal* and *hazaj* modes, each in accordance with the requisite fingering. Well, dear sir, spending your time that way is of no use whatsoever to a doctor or to the wretched patient waiting for a cure!"

5.4 In response to all this, I repeated, "I am not an oculist!"

And he retorted, "I see that you *are* someone who claims one way of life only to deny another. Come, tell me, what are you?"

"A surgeon," I replied.

"Well," he exclaimed, "that is the purview of our colleague Abū Sālim here."

Part the Sixth: In Which the Surgeon Considers the Guest's Knowledge of Anatomy and Physiology

Then the old fellow said, "Drink this round and then question him." 6.1
He then turned to the boy pouring the wine and said, "Give him a drink!" So he did, and Abū Sālim drank then recited:

"Give me a generous cup of rain mixed with wine,
 a balm for all troubles and woes,
A potent drink with a lineage
 traceable to the time of Qaḥṭān.
It cloaks the palm of its drinker
 with gleaming sparkles of gold."

The cupbearer filled the cup and gave it to him. The old fellow then said to Abū Jābir, "Sing the verses of our teacher Abū l-Ḥusayn Ibn Naffākh," so he plunged right in:

"Every wounded man can hope to be healed,
 except for a heart afflicted by her eyes!
Whenever she smiles my cheeks are soaked
 with the rain promised by the flash of her teeth."

They all drank, filled their cups once more, and sang in *hazaj*:

"My sighs arise from the heat of passion;
 he has slain my every vital organ,

Quenched his lethal thirst with my entire body,
devoured my every limb.
The healthy heap blame on the suffering
but, Lord, I would never wish him such pain!"

6.2 The whole group drank again and, signaling to me, he said, "The surgeon must be an expert in anatomy; he must know the anatomy and physiology of each limb to avoid cutting open vital flesh, severing any nerves, or damaging the muscles and various sinews." He then asked me, "How good is your knowledge of surgical procedure?"

"It is faultless," I replied.

He then asked, "How many sinews or fibers are there in the stomach?"

"Three," I replied.

"And what are they?"

I said, "One is positioned lengthways, end to end, to draw in the food; the other is lateral to keep the food in place; and the third lies obliquely in order to dispel the food."

"If," he continued, "someone were to say to you, 'No! Rather, the dispelling comes from the fiber positioned laterally, the retention is performed by the one positioned lengthwise, and the drawing in of food comes from the one placed obliquely,' how would you reply? Do you believe there is empirical evidence for this? Can the truth of it be gleaned from observed actions and effects?"

"No," I replied.

6.3 Our host then chimed in: "By God, since he thinks we treated him unfairly by preventing him from eating all this food, now he won't answer our questions!"

Abū Sālim then said, "I suppose you thought I would ask you about gaping wounds at the joints and why it is that they do not form scars and do not heal quickly. Or about the difference between male and female organs. Or what causes the delayed eruption of wisdom teeth in an elderly person. These questions never trouble elite doctors."

He then turned to the others and said, "This profession has afforded us puffed-up turbans and toques indicative of our majestic status, and adorned us with capacious capes of office and large seal rings, and the veneration that is received from common folk. When the most eminent doctors pass away, the masses ask, Oh for so-and-so! Where will the likes of such a great man come from? When will we hear of him again? Especially an individual who, with a book in his hand, twists the waxed ends of his moustache, nods, and gestures with his hands while he reads aloud. What then of the Apostles[20] who resurrect the dead and cure chronic illnesses? Or Hippocrates with his medicine? Or Archimedes with his inventions? Or Euclid with his calculations? But if you examine such a man's science and knowledge, you will find him devoid of all the claims he has arrogated to himself in order to earn a living, for he is as the poet has described:

"If ever you test his expertise, he replies,
'My knowledge, friend, is there in a basket,
Ever so carefully written in faultless notebooks.'
If you say, 'Come, tell us something!'
He scratches his beard and wipes his nose,
and when he himself is informed about something,
His jaw drops and he lets out a fart!

"If such a man bandages an injured forearm, or performs a vene- 6.4
section, or applies collyrium with a clean stylus, or examines a urine sample in a phial and shakes his head, has he paid his discipline its due, in both theory and practice? And what of it when he says, 'I have done due diligence,' when in fact he has been distracted, forgetting the dictum of Hippocrates that 'Life is short, but the art is long'; and he forgets furthermore that time flies, that movement and change are constant, that opportunities for deliverance are as fleeting as lightning bolts, that desired objectives are hit or miss, and that souls are bound to burn and melt away? If such a charlatan happens to be in the presence of a real physician who has worn himself

out by studying every night, the charlatan finds that all he needs is to be competitive and arrogant, to appeal to gullible women for help, or to appeal to common folk and to his friends to intercede on his behalf with the patient until the physician is sent packing. You know how persistently his ilk push their own brand of medicine on the patient: 'until a pasture springs up from his dung.'

6.5 "Then, when you ask him why his patient died, he says, 'He could not possibly have survived. The disease was fatal and he lacked the requisite strength. A physician can only do the best he can; it is not in the power of the profession to cure every sick person. No one would die if every patient who sought medical aid were healed! But the death of each of us is allotted by fate. What can we do, when we have no recourse and no power to lengthen a life's prescribed span! Goodness! The patient was already in terrible distress, and it does pain me so to lose him, but even prophets die—no one lives forever!'

"Then he would quote Aḥmad ibn Ḥanbal, expatiating on the state of the deceased patient and changing the subject in order to find fault with the first physician. And when asked what innovation he had introduced in his treatment, he sighed and recited:

"'He experienced the same loss that afflicted Lubad.'[21]

"And if the patient convalesced, this same charlatan would claim, 'I freed him from the jaws of a lion and rescued him from the brink of the grave,' thinking it was he who had loosened the bandage from the sick man's jaw, restrained the hand of the corpse washer, and wrested him from the grip of the angels Munkar and Nakīr when they had begun to call him to account."

6.6 The host then asked me, "Why do you let your head droop mournfully?"

"Because I am not a surgeon," I replied.

He grew angry at my shifting claims from discipline to discipline, and declaimed:

"I see you are a descendant of Moses's people,
Who could not put up with the same food every day."[22]

"You are right, sir. I usually eat three times a day."

"Well, forget that!" he said. "I did not mean to encourage you! But tell me, what are you?"

"A bloodletter," I said.

The old fellow said, "This is in the purview of our young colleague Abū Jābir. It is his turn to examine you."

Part the Seventh: The Examination of the Phlebotomist on the Requisite Knowledge of the Physiology of Venesection

Abū Jābir said to our host, "Sir, I would ask you to take my place in examining him. In return I will reward you by singing the verses Shājī dedicated to al-Mutawakkil when she presented him with her slave girl the day he was bled." 7.1

"Go ahead!"

So the young man launched into song:

"You bled a vein to stay in good health.
  May God bless you with vitality!
Drink this cup of wine, sire.
  Delight in this slave girl's voice,
And grant the woman who gave her to you
  permission to visit you an extra night."

The old fellow drank, shrieking with delight. Everyone but me filled his cup copiously, and Abū Jābir recited more verse:

"Wretched doctor who is palping your hand—
  how impudently he treated you!
If his glances were his cupping blades,
  their keenness would bleed you dry."

7.2 After downing another cup, the guests grew quiet. The old fellow now told them, "The kings of Greece would never teach a discipline without first examining a student's birth horoscope. This is because the innate talents of any man show clearly in his birth sign. Those whose birth signs they did not know were introduced into a house where illustrations of the various disciplines were displayed. They would teach them whatever their hearts and souls naturally desired:

"Every man pines for his like . . .

"Galen would deduce the ambitions of a young boy from the way he behaved with his friends in the playground, basing his judgment on whether the boy preferred to play a king or a servant. At that age, a person behaves according to his dominant nature and his animal instincts override his ability to reason.

7.3 "When this natural system of selection is corrupted, every druggist applies himself to inspecting urine samples, pontificating about natural character, and finds a market for goods he cannot sell, especially when he has spiked his medicine with a dash of sal ammoniac, dyes, soaps, cosmetics, and cubeb. Thus did Shaʿthāʾ swear on the Qurʾan to Sukaynah[23] that there was no medicine in the world better than his own. He would even boil barley water and blow on the fire to create a smoky environment—the wretch didn't know that the phlebotomist needs to take care of his eyes, treat them with pure collyrium, and drink cleansing cereal infusions. Good God, I don't know which is more lamentable: the phlebotomist pushed into a practice he knows nothing about, or his deluded patient who has placed his hand in the phlebotomist's and given him free rein over his veins."

7.4 The old fellow then said to me, "Shall I question you now?"

"Ask whatever you like," I replied.

And he said, "Do not imagine I will ask you about the various pathologies that require certain veins to be bled with a lengthwise incision, a lateral one, or an oblique one—this is well known. Nor will I ask you why cupping the vena salvatella in some pathologies is more beneficial than bleeding the vena basilica, when the former is a part of the latter. Nor about the protocols the phlebotomist should observe during, before, and after the procedure. Nor about the various veins, knowledge of which is acquired through analogies, or empirically, or by inspiration in one's sleep—even hospital rats know all that! Nor will I ask you about where to locate the vein of the forehead in an adolescent or the vein of the vertex in adults; nor about red blood that turns black or black blood that turns red when water is added to each.

"No! I will ask you instead about the reason one refrains from venesection during a full moon and why there is more blood in the bodies of living creatures when the moon is waxing than when it is waning. Do you know?" 7.5

"No," I replied.

"Well, do you know the three benefits of binding the arm before cupping?" he asked.

"No," I replied.

"Well, do you know who first signaled the benefits of cupping according to the various pathologies?" he asked.

"No."

He rebuked me, saying, "You spend your life dishonoring dinner tables. You eat, you drink, you sleep, and then writhe before the questions posed to you. You're like a vein that vanishes when the scalpel is applied to it. 7.6

"With you bleeding veins and collecting silver, all we've got is people testifying that 'So-and-so is eager to let blood and has a quick hand.' The likes of you cut into a major artery and cause fatal blood loss; you sever nerves, causing paralysis, loss of feeling, and contraction of the hand. When making incisions into a muscle, you draw impurities into the limb.

"By God, the discipline is ruined by you lot. For you, 'astute practice' means holding the arm rather than binding it as required, squeezing the vein until all the blood is drained, tugging at the bandage, crumpling the compress into a ball, and then forgetting the scalpel under the dressing. Your sort only knows how to spill blood and take the money. If someone experienced an unexpected interruption of their vital signs or if their temperature suddenly dropped, you would advise a venesection and bloodletting straightaway."

7.7 The old fellow then said, "Show me your scalpels."

I took out my instrument pouch and showed them to him. He contemplated them and said, "Where are the curved and the angular blades? Where are the lances, the obtuse blades, and the axe for the forehead? How about the needle for the temples and the ointment for stanching the wound?"

I said, "I don't have any of those."

"Well, show me your lovely fingers, then," he jeered.

When I held out my hand, he said, "These fingers aren't even any use for palping a vein. There isn't even a spark in your answers to these questions!"

"I am not a phlebotomist," I said.

"What are you, then?" he said.

"An apothecary," I replied.

"Well," said the old fellow, "that is a subject for our colleague Abū Mūsā."

Part the Eighth: The Examination of the Apothecary on the Guest's Knowledge of Remedies and Medicines

The old fellow said, "Let's drink a round; then you can examine him." 8.1

So they all took another fill. Abū Mūsā then raised his cup and said, "How beautiful the verses of Ibn al-Muʿtazz!

"A wine created by the sun
like daylight in the cup,
A breeze without a gust,
a liquid that does not course."

He then turned to the young man and said, "Sing us the song of our maestro Aḥmad ibn Qurābah," and he began to sing:

"When I joined my friends who had dozed off,
I thought there was a druggist among them.
'Whose face is this?' I asked, shaken into consciousness.
'This is your beloved, come to see you.'
'Blessed is this house with your arrival,' I said.
'Welcome to you, sweet visitor!'"

When they had drunk their wine, Abū Mūsā said, "I will not ask 8.2
you about medicines that must be used right away, or used within a month, or those that keep, no matter how long—such things are

well known. I will not ask you about the flavorless medication that turns sweet when vinegar is added to it; nor about the one that turns sour when sugar is added to it. Nor about dry powders that are softened when a rob is added to them, nor liquid medicines that solidify when water is added—all this is well known!

8.3 "Rather, I will ask you about the stone that shrinks when brought close to the light of a lamp, and about moonseed drupes, and whitebeam berries, and Indian spikenard, and zinc tutty, and which simples grow in which season—do you know about these?"

"No," I said.

"Do you know about colocynth?" he asked.

"Yes," I said.

"But can you tell the stamen from the pistil?"

"No."

"Can you distinguish the part that is medicinal and usable from the part that is deadly venom and to be discarded?"

"No."

"Do you know about plant sponges, those from the land as opposed to those from the sea?"

"No."

"Do you know when the use of wolf and lizard dung is prescribed?"

"No."

"Do you know what changes taste without changing color and vice versa? And what does both and what does neither?"

"No."

"Do you know the gemstone that is white when one first looks upon it, then as one continues to gaze seems to turn red, then violet, and finally a deep black?"

"No."

"Do you know the plain medication that is sweet, bitter, sour, and salty to the tongue, all at once?"

"No."

The old fellow said, "These are not of your devising; they are all in the lessons of Dioscorides, my dear Mandrake! Wild pennyroyals and thorny plants are fobbed off on us by dealers as the real thing. Your kind play with people's lives. But this discipline is dear to me; even those who can describe it or know anything about it are scarce or nonexistent. Merchants now are loath to import these products, so all that is left to the apothecary are merely rows of earthenware pots, ornamental trays, shops decorated with dark-painted doors, premises full of scales, measures, sieves, filters, and washbasins. Now all we care about is the quality of henna, rosewater, dark dyes, zinc sulfate lotions, lyes, sal ammoniac, laxatives, and Mother Mary's incense. As Shaʿthāʾ said to al-ʿĀtikah, 'The incense of Abū l-Ḥusayn the druggist is out of this world,' and as ʿUlayyah the midwife says, 'Where can we find salves the likes of his?,' and as Sukaynah the hairdresser says, 'Nobody beats his analgesic cream!'—she swears his ointments are beyond compare, all the more so because when she asks him, 'How much exfoliating soap can you give me for five dirhams?' he gives her more than she pays for, swearing he would never take the full price from her. He sends her off with her goods, having made for her one of the nets with which to 'trap' his livelihood. There is not a single bathhouse, judge's gathering, tailor's shop, or cloth merchant's premises that doesn't speak effusively of the qualities of Abū l-Ḥusayn the druggist." 8.4

When he had had his say, I could not answer him and thought to make my peace with him. "Sir," I said, "the Ancients say that alms are due for every blessing: for wealth it is to give charity to the needy; for power it is to protect the weak and the oppressed; for eloquence it is to argue on behalf of those who cannot; for influence it is to protect those who have none; for knowledge it is to teach those who have no learning. Disbursing charity is required of those who possess wealth, even though this has a negative effect on the principal. Isn't it essential, then, to disburse knowledge, since doing so enriches everyone? Likewise, it has been said that knowledge is 8.5

like a head of hair, which will grow more vigorously after it has been cut or shaven. One only has a certain amount of hair: it will grow back more amply if shaven but stay the same if left alone. Can you respond to these statements?"

8.6 The old fellow said, "Anyone who refuses to offer wisdom to those in search of it is like a person who refuses to give cool, sweet water to the thirsty; whereas someone who offers wisdom to those not in search of it is like a person offering warm and briny water to a man whose thirst has already been slaked. I will respond to every one of these statements after you have told me what profession you claim for yourself! I'll then give you a lesson as exquisite as fine embroidery and purified gold."

"I am a man who came to these parts with a load of books," I replied.

"So," he said, "you are a peddler of assorted scraps!"

He then turned to his guests and announced, "He's just like that other young man we had dealings with!"

"Who was that?" I asked.

Part the Ninth: Concerning Slanderous Doctors who are Scornful of the Sick

The old fellow answered, "He was a youth who grew up among us. 9.1
He went by Jārūf Abū l-Wafā'.[24] One evening after recovering from an illness, he began to claim he was a doctor.

"God said to him, 'Become a physician
and destroy people!
Take sick men's money—that's excusable—
and send him to the grave.'

"God protect us and you from the misfortunes wrought by his hands.

"He took to wearing striped and gilded clothes, and rings set with gems of hyacinth and amethyst. I felt sorry for him, all the same.

"It is misfortune enough
that a man's enviers feel sorry for him!

"I felt sorry at the scorn he provoked in others, since his dress code made them hostile to his professional arrogance and provoked them to slander; they accused him of things I swear he would never think of doing. He was not content to be like us, miserable doctors, satisfied just as a bird is with feathers in place of clothing or as a beast is with hooves in place of footwear. That is preferable and more beneficial.

"We let the game play out. We are, good sir, just like the venerable and ascetic doctors of old. All the habits that differ from our forefathers are effectively usurped. We are, God preserve you, content with a diet of bread stew and our basic health. It is a problem when a poor invalid sees a doctor in the garb of a vizier—how can the patient be comfortable enough to let him see his spittle and urine and excrement? But he was still a young man and had no shame and no sense that he should not let his lofty position make him insolent.

9.2 "It is well known that the intelligent man should be immovable in demeanor, just like a mighty mountain unshaken by severe winds. An idiot is like grass moved by the faintest breeze. Social graces rid the intelligent man of intemperance but only cause it to increase in an idiot, just as day brings light to those with sight but renders a bat even blinder than it already is.

9.3 "It amazed me when someone told me that this chap, whom I had known as an orphan, was a doctor. As a young man, he began to frequent pretentious folk who encouraged his desire to join the cavalry, and this lasted a good while. I lost track of him until I heard that he had begun to wear a turban, manicure his nails, dress like a grandee, and wait on the gentry, having learned to read and write and spread salacious stories about the affairs of other doctors.

9.4 "I remember him telling the following story to a group of governors—although he made numerous grammatical errors in the telling. He recounted how one of the caliph's concubines had complained to Jibrīl ibn Bukhtīshūʿ of her master's bad breath. Jibrīl advised her to have some tailors sew musk into the seams of her gowns. That way, when her master slept with her she could turn to her seams and smell their fragrance. If the stench was too strong, she could rely on her seams. She did this first with one seam, then two, then three . . . People burst out laughing at the way he had told the story to their host and at the fact that he seemed not to know the difference between masculine and feminine verbs.

9.5 "How different this story is from what took place between Isḥāq ibn Ḥunayn and al-Muʿtaḍid's minister, al-Qāsim ibn ʿUbaydullah.

Al-Qāsim heard that Isḥāq had drunk a laxative. They were friends and al-Qāsim wanted to tease him, so he wrote to him as follows:

"'Tell me, how was your night?
What state were you in?
How many times did the camel
carry you to the latrine?'

"Isḥāq wrote back:

"'I was well and very happy,
relaxed in the extreme!
The ride and the camel
were to an empty latrine;
Your concern is the height of kindness—
you're the object of all my hopes!'

"How different our wretched young friend was to some of the charming and articulate doctors in the military. One doctor was sent to the army by his master, and when he returned he was asked facetiously about the battle he had witnessed. He answered, 'When the two sides met on a field, it looked like a hospital courtyard. Had a scalpel been hurled, there's no doubt it would have struck me. In ten heartbeats our enemies suffered a fatal setback in the course of their illness, and we returned in perfect health to the presence of your well-balanced humors!'"

The old fellow then said, "These fine physicians are dear to me, 9.6
by God. But such people have died off. The specialists of our various disciplines have perished, as have the evaluators of our science. The very essence of our vocation has been extirpated along with its practitioners. Its spinal column has been severed. There is no breach of our tenets that isn't considered licit, and no virtue that isn't defiled. The calamity is universal, solace the exception. This is because the sick will pass away even if there is a doctor present: there is an impenetrable curtain separating the quack and proper treatment. This is all patently obvious and requires no further evidence or proof."

9.7 The guests then replenished their cups, and Abū Sālim called for an extra-big cup. When it was full, he raised it and said, "How wonderful are the verses by Abū Nuwās about wine cups:

"We fill with wine cups like stars,
constellations in our hands,
Rising as the server makes his rounds
and setting within us when the stars set."

He then said to Abū Jābir, "Lad, sing one of my songs," and he sang:

"The evil eye of fate has struck us.
Would it had not looked upon us
and afflicted us with all manner of suffering.
I used to take pity on my eyes and weep,
but now anyone dear to me
has already been humbled."

They all became enraptured and rowdy, drinking and filling their cups. The host suggested another song to Abū Jābir, who sang:

"She was sick, so I visited her—then she sang!
Now she was like the visitor, I the patient.
By God, if every heart was as hard as hers
no parent would feel pity for their sickly child!"

9.8 They continued to drink, blessing one another, and pouring thanks upon their host. When they had quieted down, I asked, "Sir, who exactly is the doctor whose conduct you were describing?"

He laughed and said, "He was a young man I got to know in Baghdad. He used to drink from dried-up puddles instead of fresh water. Now he dines off delicately peeled broad beans and finely strained eggplant. As the old poet said:

"When clothed, a man forgets he was ever naked,
that he was ever a guttersnipe when money fills his pockets,
That he ever felt misery when, of an evening,
he courts a beauty with kohl-lined languorous eyes.

"However, he felt that a lavish life still escaped him and that the recognition of lofty status continued to elude him, so he trespassed upon a métier that was not his:

> "No one should take offense at God's blessings,
> though people often find the outcome repugnant.

"I followed his development, thinking that the passage of time would smooth his rough edges. However, he felt times were treating him well. He pursued all kinds of gain and hustled for money, always adapting to his victims, be they soldiers or merchants or whoever, peddling medicines to anyone and everyone: dental creams for the young, fertility drugs for women, drops for old men's failing eyes, and hair dyes for elderly women. At times he would practice medicine, at others he would rely on astrology; sometimes he would coddle his patients and other times act as a middleman. He would tinker with potions as though he were ʿAbd Allāh ibn Hilāl: first using solvents, then binding agents, and always studying the outcome closely.[25] All the while he traded in shrouds and coffins, renting out funeral clothing, seeking profit from those in mourning, sidling up to those who stood to inherit from the deceased. He would never visit a household without leaving in his wake a trail of dishonor and shame to the profession. He took pleasure in the distress of the sick and was distressed when they recovered at his decrepit hands. Humanity was his enemy and the gravediggers and vultures that circled above them his friends. 9.9

> "These birds grew used to him and trusted him,
> following him to every location.

"In the spring he was in cahoots with a perfume seller he knew, 9.10
and arranged to pocket half the profits from the sale of medicines. He spent his time visiting the heads of households in their homes and visiting merchants in their shops. As spring ended, he issued stark warnings about the onset of the hot season, and in the autumn about the onset of winter. He once encountered a certain Hind. 'I

see you have changed,' he said, to which she replied, 'What can relieve the misery that has afflicted me?' 'It's as if you've been victim to the evil eye.' 'Uncle,' she replied, 'it's on account of the severity with which Wālid Abī l-Faḍl treats me, God take him! I swear, if I took my afflictions to heart, I'd be dead already.' 'His mind has deteriorated, good lady,' he replied, 'and he's become confused. But, God willing, he trusts you in his heart. If he was afflicted solely as everyone else is these days, he would know your value. Do you really think he could find someone else as beautiful as you? I have visited people's houses and have never seen anyone more fetching than you.' He would talk to her like this and instructed her in infidelity. He led her into adultery and got her to slap and mistreat her husband. Then he told her, 'God curse the world and these fleeting moments of deception, such as yours, good lady,' and recited:

"'My world consists of my soul alone.
I don't want anyone to survive me,
And when I'm gone, let the sun set,
never to rise again.

9.11 "'Good lady, will you accept my advice?' he said.

"'Yes, uncle. I will not question you, sir.'

"He said, 'You should drink whey—it makes the body fertile, fattens you where you are skinny, gives you a fair complexion, adds color to your face, softens your skin, strengthens your appetite, improves your digestion, sweetens your breath, and rids you of blotches on your skin.' He then examined her and said, if she hoped to conceive a child, 'Let us give you something else so that we have a child whom al-Qaysī, your husband, will look after.'

"How often did he guarantee that she would conceive a boy, and he stuck to her until she was convinced the whey had made her fertile, brought on her pregnancy, and restored her husband's love for her. He insistently prescribed strange medicines for her and told her to go to a particular druggist. 'He is a difficult person,' he would say, 'but his wares are excellent. Do not give a thought to the costs.' He told his assistant, 'He will demand twenty dirhams and then reduce the cost by five; but try to get them for ten. If he agrees—which I doubt he will—then that's a good price. Do as you see fit, but do not come back without settling the matter as tomorrow the moon will be in Scorpio. Wish him a good morning for me and tell him I'll make it up to him with another purchase, even though he'll make no profit on this sale because it is meant for a friend.'

"If the servant bought from another druggist, he would be like a lion who let his prey escape and, seeing it, is ravenous.

"He said, 'Where are the myrobalan, camel thorn, and fresh barberries? You have a tendency to buy cheap fare. Don't you know that the Ancients said that if the physician is smart, the patient willing, the servant empathetic, and the medicine good, the illness will not linger? God knows, I have not drawn a veil across the truth and have accepted no bribe where medicine is concerned, and I use only the best concoctions. If you want my advice, take it, or you'll be prey to swindlers.'

"He did all this while complaining about unemployment and the challenges of making a living."

"What you've told me about this man fascinates me," I said. 9.12

And he said, "Well, I've only told you the least despicable stories:

"Forget those other things I could tell you.
If I told them I could not restore our trust.

"If malice weren't abhorrent to me, I could punish him for all the unseemly acts he perpetrated at my expense."

"What else did he do?" I asked.

"Let's drink another cup and I'll tell you."

Part the Tenth: A Defense of the Devoted Doctor and a Denigration of the One Who Displaced Him

They filled their goblets and the young musician launched into song: 10.1

> "The doctor felt my hand in an ignorant way and I said,
> 'Away with you—this is the critical day.'
> 'What is troubling you?' he asked.
> 'I am suffering from love for a neighbor,' I replied.
> He stood there, amazed, and said,
> 'An ailing person whose cure is another person!'"

And then he recited:

> "You have a sickness no doctor can cure:
> you suffer from the dandiness of a joker."

When they had drunk their fill, our host said to me, "Good sir, 10.2
listen to this story. I had a patient whose condition worried me, so I stayed by his side day and night, observing his behavior, watching for signs of his illness, gauging their relative strength and weakness, and tracking his various symptoms, good and bad. I examined his urine samples and compared the various residues, one consistency against the other, one color against the other—all this to be able to discern the end of the onset of his illness, its worsening and its eventual decline. My goal was to use the right medicine at the right time, and not to find myself on one path, so to speak, and the disease on

another. I didn't want to be like a dentist who pulls out a healthy molar instead of the one that has decayed.

10.3 "I monitored his medications, liquids, plasters, and air quality, because a doctor needs the courage of a soldier joining battle when he sees a patient, having prepared all manner of things for his own protection and for combat. He does not know his enemy, after all, neither the weapons he uses nor the ambushes he is planning. So it is with a doctor: When he visits a patient he must know the constitution of his body, the state of his limbs and organs, the ailments that can afflict them—their causes, their treatment, the medications that can cure them, and the substitute medications in case the primary treatment is not available. He must know how to produce them and how they are to be applied, cognizant of the equivalence between symptom and dose, and how to make adjustments according to their properties.

"The young man in question imposed himself on my patient, asking his visitors questions, and requesting prescriptions from friends to the point that my patient dispensed with my services and engaged him as his principal physician. God knows, this came as a relief to me as well as to his servants and to the apothecaries with whom I had been dealing!

10.4 "I was not jealous, but you would not believe me if I were to say that I was not furious. As the saying goes, 'The most aggrieved is the one supplanted by one less worthy.' But this kind of mistreatment has through the ages tormented so many colleagues in this profession. The way an incompetent man attains his goal is exactly how the resolute expert is kept from his objective. In any event, they say a decent person leaves in good faith when his path is blocked. It is best to forbear when there is no hope of changing a situation and when all patience has been exhausted.

> "How can I be patient when I observe
> my enemies tipping the scales against my success?

"I now believe that this upstart doctor is like a ninety-five-year-old who has never properly treated a patient. He knows no rules and has never plowed the field of medicine. He treads another path completely and knows nothing of the manner in which doctors tend to their patients. Nothing of the kind has ever occurred to him: he has neither heard of our ways nor thought to practice properly. 10.5

"If you believe all this, it might seem to you that I'm defaming him. But after I left, I heard that this charlatan did alter my treatment; he did not follow my procedures, choosing instead to show off his own method. The patient is without question in a terrible state, but people in our time get the doctors they deserve, like this one, cunning and wretched.

"I have heard he will not even speak to someone without weighing the money due to him. How different he is from us, we who consider the sick to be our children and our brethren. Heavens! If you were to see me at prayer, you would see something truly amazing. As you know, some implore God for abundant wealth and others for a virtuous death. As for me, I stretch out my hands and ask for a clear urine sample, normal saliva, plentiful perspiration, copious urination, and healthy defecation. During my late-night prayer, I beseech: 'Lord, when my patient so-and-so suffers delirium tonight, may he sweat copiously, and as for so-and-so, who suffers from gout, bless him with restful sleep.'" 10.6

"Sir," I said, "perhaps you should ask God to provide you with a livelihood that will eliminate the need for this." 10.7

The old fellow laughed and said, "You're like the man who suffers from colic and spends his night asking God to bless him with flatulence, but when he despairs of any relief his last resort is to beseech, 'Lord, grant me Paradise.' His doctor will say, 'You spent the whole night asking God for a fart and He didn't answer and now you ask for Paradise, the heavens, and the earth! You could have signaled to me what you prayed for—and if my prayers were answered you would be saved. Instead, the patient for whom I wished the reprieve of diarrhea still suffers from colic and the one for whom I wished a purgative sweat is afflicted remorselessly with fever. The reason these supplications fail is that people pay us nothing, so we pray without purity of intention.'

10.8 "God protect us from the stagnant practice of doctors and the sincerity of the sick. All the same, I have had discussions with this scoundrel, as he knows full well and cannot deny. For instance, I asked him one day in jest, 'Why are a dog's feces useful in the tanning process, a cow's dung useful in the fuller's craft, a wolf's droppings useful in the treatment of diphtheria, and a lizard's excrement useful in the healing of ulcers?' My questions left him speechless. I took the opportunity to vex him with another question: 'Why is mere water sufficient to clean one's hand after defecating despite the repugnance of excrement, and yet after a good meal the odor of food can only be purged with water scented with perfume or with a detergent of sedge and alkali?' 'I don't know,' he replied. 'Why,' I asked, 'does urine tend to thicken and become cloudy when cold whereas fruit juices become clear and flow freely?'

10.9 "He interrupted me and began to grind his teeth, regretting his misspent youth, when his wood was still green and supple and his clay still ductile and malleable. He felt the remorse of the young man mentioned by Galen."

"What young man?" I asked.

And he answered, "Galen said that a young man whose beauty distracts him from study and who is abandoned by his loved ones when he has lost his looks will cry out in remorse, 'I wish I had never been handsome!'"

"Sir, can you not patch up the damage done to your relationship?" I asked.

"Not all diseases have a remedy!" he answered. "How often our influential men have tried to mend our differences, but clumsy prodding never put a dislocated hip back in its socket. Things will never be as before! Many patients have tried to resolve our differences, but without knowing the underlying truth of what had passed between us. Such effort is fruitless, like stitching up just one side of an infected lesion. The wound that lies between us is deep and has never been cleansed, aired, then treated. Sometimes it heals over, but it's infected and the scab won't last. The relapse is worse than the original affliction. We'd ignore each other for ages, and then he would talk to me again, hiding his hatred:

"One day, he sought reconciliation,
 but failed in his attempt.
Any wound will reopen after a time
 if it is not cleaned before treatment.

"How I pretended not to see so many things, straining to forget what had transpired! I would say to myself, 'Perhaps . . .' or 'Maybe . . .' And I would interpret things favorably, remembering what the Ancients said: 10.10

"Your scolding may well have good effect—
 how often bodies benefit from their illness.

"But he would go back to his vile ways. I would send him packing but he would return 'in peace,' seeking friendship, ignorant of the fact that it is foolish to seek amicability in bad faith—that's like seeking women's affections with crude and vulgar behavior:

"Either be a true friend
 so I can tell virtue from vice,
Or cast me off and make me your enemy,
 and we can be forever wary of each other.

"I would listen but stay silent, ignoring him while I worked, not taking notice of him until he struck me with invective. He did not realize that a tree felled with an axe can grow again, that a scalpel causes a flesh wound that heals, but a wound caused by the tongue never heals or scars over. The arrowheads of angry words may penetrate the flesh and be extracted but the arrowheads of words that penetrate the heart can never be extracted. Every fire can be extinguished—a blaze with water, poison with an antidote, sorrow 10.11

with forbearance, passion with solace—but the fire of hatred never abates. This man planted a tree of animosity between us; if he were not so shameless and self-absorbed, he could occupy himself with treating his own disorder—the returns for him would be far greater. As the saying goes, 'If there is a funeral procession in your neighborhood but you have no flour in your house and your children are hungry, do not join the procession or feel obliged to console your neighbors: your affliction is greater than theirs.'"

10.12 "What is wrong with him?" I asked.

And he replied, "Forget this man. Instead, seek God's protection from the vicissitudes of time. God knows I could tell you about his unimaginably wicked acts, were he not like a son to me and were I not averse to maligning him behind his back. Let's stop talking about him—let's not be backbiters."

"God forbid," I said, "that we should be guilty of slander, but there is one thing I would like to ask."

"Ask away," he said.

And I asked, "Who did this young man study with?"

"With the most illustrious people to have set foot on this soil," he replied. "With men imbued with the science of the Ancients. But what good is an efficient cause in the absence of receptive matter? It was like writing on water—every line vanishes. And yet his teacher read with him and taught him to the point of fatigue and exhaustion.

10.13 "You should know that there are three categories of backward students in this profession. The first reads profusely but nothing is imprinted in his mind—he is like a convalescing patient who thinks he will benefit from overeating, ignorant of the fact that that he needs healthy limbs and organs to absorb the food and put on weight: he eats avidly but his body remains unchanged. The second reads a lot but understands little; he is like a glutton whose consumption bloats his figure, which diminishes his strength and makes his limbs heavy. Such an ignoramus is of two kinds: one knows where he stands and therefore does not seek advancement, fully aware of his deficiencies, limiting himself to prescribing pips and oxymel. The other is proud in his ignorance, yet is like a swollen scholar who is clearly overweight and struggles as a result:

> "A man may dress elegantly,
> but denuded he is just a wretch.
> So too a person with rosy cheeks
> may suffer from inflamed lungs.

10.14 "This is why Galen said, 'Ignorance of one's own ignorance is ignorance twice over.' Suppose we concede that he is indeed learned; what good is that without the ability to practice? They say there is nothing more damaging for a patient than a physician who talks a good game but cannot actually practice. A practitioner who finds it hard to articulate his diagnosis may in fact have the talent and experience, while a charlatan who elicits admiration with his eloquence and good manners may produce unwelcome consequences. Any doctor who relies in his treatment on affected speech and who spouts excuses when the patient risks dying without the appropriate care is like a man who drinks poison wittingly and relies on having the antidote. It is patently clear that sound knowledge is only realized in good practice. The sick man who knows the remedy for his illness does not profit from his knowledge if he fails to take the remedy: for him, neither respite nor recovery—quite the contrary!"

10.15 The old fellow then turned to his apprentice and said, "We have been sidetracked from our pleasures by the mention of this young charlatan. Come, give me my cup."

They all filled their vessels, and he proposed that Abū Jābir sing the following:

> "Aḥmad asked, not knowing what ailed me,
> "Utbah, do you truly love life?'
> I sighed and replied, 'Yes! My love for it
> flows in every vein,
> But my physician and family
> are all weary of my suffering.

If only I could die and find peace.
As long as I live, there will be no relief.'"

He sang while they drank and made merry. Then the young man sang the following verses:

"You afflict me with your absence.
You torture me, keeping your guard.
You deprive me of sleep,
shunning me as you do.
Why not show a generous spirit
to one you've tormented so,
To one the doctor has failed
and wept over?"

10.16 Our host then cried out, "By the Healer of all wounds, the one Who causes blood to flow in our veins! If these words were inscribed with a needle in the corner of the eye, what a sight that would be!" The group rose, drank while standing, and toasted the host's health.

The old fellow seemed more relaxed, so I seized the opportunity, sidled up to him, and asked, "Would you fill a cup for me—to drive away hardship and to let me partake of the delights you are sharing with this company?"

"If you show yourself deserving," he replied.

"How can I show that I am?" I asked.

"By answering me this," he said. "After which of the two breaths do you drink—exhalation or inhalation? And when you drink, is your heart beat synchronized with the peristalsis or not?"

So I held my breath to determine the answer and he exclaimed, "This is just like what Ibn Qutaybah wrote about in *Conduct of the Secretaries*, about people who were once asked how many teeth they had and all responded by putting their hands into their mouths to count them!

10.17 "I asked you an easy question, not when the fetus's pulse is in sync with its pregnant mother and when it's not, nor whether the systolic beat occurs before the diastolic. I didn't ask you why when people open their mouths wide they blow out hot air, warming cold things, but if they purse their lips they blow out cold air and cool hot things; nor did I ask you why a person's breath stokes large fires but puts out small ones. Nor will I ask you why the rhythmic movements of the veins and the heart are in sync, yet distinct from the movement of respiration."

And then he asked, "Do you know anything about this?"

"No," I said.

"Do you know that the benefit of inhaling is, specifically, to breathe in fresh air, and, accidentally, to take in liquids such as water, wine, broth, and steeped dates, and to sniffle mucus and smell pleasant odors?"

"No," I said.

"And do you know that the benefit of exhaling is, specifically, to let out hot air, to blow, and, accidentally, to call out to animals, to speak, cough, play wind instruments, kindle fire by blowing on it, belch, spit, gasp, and expel bad odors? That together, inhaling and exhaling allow one to yawn, laugh, cry, sigh, say 'Ugh,' and sneeze?"

"No," I said.

"Have one cup. I do this out of pity for you."

So I poured myself a cup. The shaykh remarked, "An expert pour! 10.18
Filled to the brim, just like the scholars who crowd the margins of their notebooks." "On the contrary," I replied, "I've 'lined' it all the way down to the bottom." He grew annoyed at this, and shouted, "You imbecile! Spheroid objects are not described by lines—only circles and arcs!" He snatched the cup from my hand and downed it. "The companionship of an ignoramus is like fever to the soul," he muttered, and then recited:

"There is intimacy in gathering
only among birds of a feather.
The ignorant man hurts me with his bad manners
just as coughing hurts those who are drinking.

"Al-Mutanabbī has said something similar:

"Suffering the offenses of a man in plain view
is like consuming rancid food that emaciates the body.

"How excellent the words of the Persian sage: 'Avoiding the ignorant is as good as associating with the learned.'"

10.19 And he went on, moved by the spirit of the moment, and asked, "Who will take over this profession after us? The art of Hippocrates and the medical sciences in general are long gone, leaving only shriveled limbs, balding eyelashes, a disfigured frame, and epiphoric eyes. Now when a physician visits a patient, he has simple choices: venesection if a long time has elapsed since the procedure was last performed, or not doing so if only a short time has elapsed since the last such intervention; or the choice between giving him a laxative if he is constipated or something to control diarrhea; or of cooling him down if he has a fever and warming him up if he has the chills; or to prepare him for the worst if he is anxious or comfort him with news of a healthy recovery if he is found to be calm and reposed. All these choices stem from the fact that the poor physician does not actually know that anxiety is often more beneficial than tranquility; that confusion is better than lucidity; that discoloration of the extremities is a better indicator of health than a radiant skin tone; and that the doctor should often administer a laxative to a patient suffering the runs in order to constipate him, and an antidiarrheal to a constipated man to loosen his bowels; and that the best way to treat a febrile condition is with foods having a hot complexion, just as foods with a cold complexion are best for lethargy; one may also treat a man with remedies that weaken his senses and general strength."

Part the Eleventh: The Public's Denigration of the Medical Profession and the Riposte

"If physicians had not shown themselves so incapable of practicing the medical arts, the common people would not have come to disparage them as they do, citing as testimony of their ineptitude popular poems and sayings, coining pejorative truisms and poetic aphorisms about them and their abilities, such as: 11.1

"How can a physician die of the same disorder
he previously treated in others as a banal sickness?
All have perished: doctor, patient,
retailer, buyer, and seller of the medication.

"Another poet said:

"People blame the doctor,
yet his failing is simply fate's affliction.

"Some will pare down the problem and say, 'By God, it is all babbling nonsense; what I know is that a man of thirty was not fated to die at twenty.' He says this ignorant of the fact that this fatalist way of thinking has killed off a hundred thousand souls. 11.2

"Another will say, 'Death is a path one must inevitably walk—physicians are simply palliatives for anguished hearts.' This in answer to those who claim that a physician is a guarantee of a long life and that medicine cures all ailments.

"Another will say, 'Why should I torture myself with dietary restrictions? When doctor so-and-so puts you on a diet, it only makes you sicker and more jaundiced.' The fool is ignorant of the fact that he would die if he didn't diet.

"Another will say, 'I eat and drink, avoid all medical treatment, and rely on God alone.' The same person accepts the advice of the veterinarian when his donkey falls ill, even though by extension he should ignore the vet and rely on God alone. The fact is, physicians who prescribe treatment do not preclude reliance on God.

"Another will say, 'How often I have been sick and gotten better without medication.' But he says this without knowing that if he had sought medical advice he would have recovered more quickly and that there will come a time when his strength will not avail him in fighting off sickness—it will be too late for the physician's intervention and he will die.

"Another will say, 'How often I have taken a treatment and dieted, and yet only recovered after eating to my heart's content.' He is unaware that his gluttony simply coincided with the end of the sickness, so he recovered. But many people have taken to gluttony before the end of their malady and have died as a result."

He then recited:

"Senseless people chide the doctor
  but their words cause him no injury.
It does no harm to the rising sun
  that the blind man cannot see it.

11.3 "When they hear a physician pronounce that a certain food is harmful, the groups who deny the benefits of the medical arts reply that they have eaten it on many occasions without any harm. They do not realize that the natural constitution protects the body as much as it can, but that it reaches a point when it can no longer protect itself, so it falls ill and perishes.

"They say that as long as there is bread in the bakery nothing can harm us. If the Grim Reaper comes along, he gets nothing. They call bread life and the baker the giver of life. And they call death the Grim Reaper. If you tell them an antidote will cure a snakebite, they reply, 'Here's the antidote and here's the viper; whoever is right, let him prove it.' If you mention the pulse, they say, 'Here are two women, one of whom is pregnant, the other sterile: diagnose their conditions based on their pulses.' They want nothing less from the physician than to be as knowledgeable as God.

"They are not convinced by what is clear and obvious to the 11.4
physician because they do not understand that this art is contingent upon many factors, but when aided by divine intervention its efficacy becomes self-evident. Just because its rules and principles are not always obvious or applicable to each patient does not mean they should be cast aside and rejected—they enable a middle ground between achievement and failure. Just because some sick people have died does not mean one should ignore medicine altogether, just as it is not the case that because some patients have recovered one should always rely on medical attention for recovery. Good sense requires that one situate oneself in the middle ground, such that those who have been saved from their affliction and regained their health should thank God Almighty. This is why even Hippocrates found it difficult to make accurate judgments about an illness's prognosis.

"When they see a doctor consulting a book, they say disparagingly, 'Does this contain a cure against death?' If he replies, 'No,' they say, 'These books contain nothing but old wives' tales spouted by feebleminded old women.' Knowledge does not increase the life of a wise man, nor does ignorance decrease it. It's as the physician Ibn Ghassān put it:

> "The nature of the cup of death
> is that the stupid and the brilliant have an equal share.

The idiot takes his place in the ground
just as the smart person does.
They rot, bereft of all their qualities,
essential or accidental.
Their animal existence is annihilated,
just as is their intellect.

11.5 "Such talk is utterly blasphemous, corrupt, and worthless. The equality of people in life and death is not an argument against immortality or against the echelons of existence in the hereafter. People may be equals when they travel together, but upon their return home they dress in finery according to their rank and based on their riches and wealth. This succinctly explains the matter and suffices to make our point.

"They place veterinary science above medicine because they have intimate knowledge of animals—which, indeed, they resemble. When they see an inkwell, they call it the amulet of shame and the treasure house of the medical profession. This is because when they see a physician poring over his books, they say his intelligence is partner to his poverty. If he speaks in careful detail about a medical matter, they say, 'He is a fool,' because they believe that knowledge can make one go mad. If they do not understand what he is saying, they say, 'This is heresy.' And if one faction supports him, the other faction recites:

"What good are education and science
when their beneficiaries acquire them but die in the end?

11.6 "They do not say that foods are hot or cold; rather: 'This one "leans,"' by which they mean it changes its nature, like a watermelon; or 'This food in its nature is prone to die,' by which they mean it is cold and dry; and they call what is humid 'tender'; they say apricots 'have the nature of fever,' and that chestnuts 'have the nature of colic.' All these statements are approximations. But the greatest disaster is their belief that camphor and ice are both hot, that fennel and henna are both cold, and that barley water 'has the nature of jaundice.'

"All this arises from the feebleness of physicians and their lack of acquaintance with the books of the Ancients. The art of medicine has all but gone extinct and has been shaken to its very roots; it has not been fortified by its developments and has perished just like the proverbial might of Sheba. People have come to disparage it and it has vanished. There are no decent doctors left, and now the midwives and those who draw up astrological charts pretend to be physicians. Its sheen has gone the way of its glory days. It has become a surplus no one needs. Hippocratic medicine has no value, and has been replaced by a new medicine that was not communicated by true Ancient practitioners at God's behest."

While he was talking, a sick man knocked at the front door, and 11.7
the old fellow allowed him in. He greeted everyone, sat down, and asked for permission to describe what ailed him. He was invited to speak and said, "My mouth feels dry; I have wind in my belly; I'm generally constipated, though, and I have phlegm in my stomach; liquid leaks onto my pillow when I sleep; a burning sensation flares up when I drink cold fluids, but most of my pains are appeased when I drink hot liquids; I laugh so much I begin to cry; I have few hopes and little joy; I eat plentifully but cannot digest, and my insides burn; my urine is as white as cotton, but if I complain about my ailments to the physicians, some of them say that I am mad, while others just stand there and shake their heads in wonder."

The old fellow said, "This is what we were talking about! You're 11.8
quite right in everything you say; it is a disease that benefits from early treatment with heat; there are causes for everything you have mentioned, but it would take a while to explain, and would require a calm constitution and clear head. Go! Stick to your diet and come back again."

He bid us farewell and left. Meanwhile, the old fellow beckoned to his student and asked him to sing, which he promptly did:

> "The blessing of sleep and the beloved's apparition
> have brought us back together.

The guardian himself would have assisted us
were it not that her bracelets and anklets sufficed."

11.9 The old fellow looked at him angrily and admonished him, saying, "We can't take you anywhere! Are these verses in line with the propositions of today's doctors and the compositions of the Ancients? Don't you know it is bad form for a singer to sing about the harvest in July?

"By God, let the rain stop—
an abundance of water does nothing but harm!

"And bad form for him to sing the following in the evening:

"Greet the morning with a face reflecting wine
and the star of good fortune.

"And bad form for him to sing this at weddings:

"How good life was at the time we parted—
though we were faithful, Fate betrayed us.

"And bad form for him to sing this to a descendant of the Prophet:

"The Crucifixion is the time for you to have fun.
For us, it's the Persian New Year festivities!"

11.10 He then said, "Sing one of those songs I suggested when I first started getting drunk." And the boy sang a piece by al-ʿAbbās ibn al-Aḥnaf in a lyric meter, plucking with his ring finger:

"They claimed she had a fever;
may God test this claim!
She complained she was in tip-top condition,
just as the moon might complain when full.
I wish I could suffer sickness like you, my lady;
you are rewarded even if your malady lasts an eternity."

The whole company drank, filled their cups again, and listened as he sang another song:

"My fever-struck darling, I'd give my life for you.
You are my only pleasure in this world.
I was sick already; your sickness only added to it.
Your affliction has become my own.
If only I could unburden you of it,
so our two sicknesses could unite as one."

Abū Ayyūb the oculist went into raptures and said, "My friends, my brethren of purity,[26] and all remaining scholars! By the Lord who created the whole natural order, if this were carved with scalpels on our ears, it would have the most wonderful effect." 11.11

They all drank, enraptured. The old fellow was particularly drunk, and as the effects of the intoxicating wine spread through his limbs and head, he became seriously incoherent and began to reveal his sorrows.

"My brother," he said, "I have grown tired amassing all scientific knowledge, and have exhausted myself reading books. Medicine has in fact never brought me the promised benefits. The reason is that valor has fallen by the wayside; men's souls have become mean and petty. Life has passed me by. I am old and will soon fall off the perch. I have no offspring to keep my reputation alive and no close friend to grieve at my grave."

He then paraphrased one of the Ancients:

"I recalled who grieved for me and remembered
only fellow physicians and my books shedding a tear."

He lowered his eyes and wept for a while. In the meantime, his guests left.

Part the Twelfth: The Conclusion of the Book and a Return Visit Rebuffed

His apprentice Abū Jābir stayed behind. The old fellow turned to his servant boy and ordered him to fill his cup and bade Abū Jābir to sing the following verses: 12.1

> "The shepherd dies with his ignorance
>
> just as Galen did with his knowledge.
>
> If he had lived longer,
>
> perhaps he would still be watching over his flock."

Then the old fellow fell on his side, fast asleep. I stood up, but when I made to leave, the servant boy asked, "Are you leaving me and this young man, sir, when we are hungry? He has spent the day singing his voice hoarse." 12.2

"Why will you go hungry," I answered, "when there is plenty of food in the house?"

"If you leave," he said, "I do not dare to disturb the old fellow and subject myself to his wrath. If you stay, you can be my pretext and we will be protected by you."

At this, I felt an urge to feed these two men and drink with them. I was piqued by the old fellow's avarice and furious at his miserliness. The servant boy brought the tray back into the room and offered up the lamb. We ate every morsel, leaving nothing. Then we turned our attention to the *fālūdhaj*, finished it off, and leaned toward the wine to drink the dregs. The young boy sang:

"I was told the fire was kindled after you left, Kulayb,
and then I sang to the guests.
They talked about matters of import.
If you'd witnessed them, you would not have despaired."

12.3 There we were, all of us drunk and having a good time, when the old fellow woke up. He raised his head, and when he saw that his trays were emptied of their meats and sweets, he asked, "What is this liberality and invasion of my household—this ransacking of my food and wine?"

"I remembered what you said when I first arrived," I said.

"What was that?" he asked.

"I make my guest laugh even before he dismounts;
he feels abundance in my presence no matter how barren the place."

"Wicked people," he said, "group together just as flies swarm around the foul parts of the body."

"Sir," I said, "we only ate a bit of your food, though we could have eaten it all."

"Plato was right," he responded, "when he said the wicked only raise your hopes. Don't you know that Isfahani kohl is imported by the camel load but is soon gone because it's all the rage?"

"Sir, you invited me to your house," I said. "You offered me food and drink—I was no burdensome gate-crasher; I didn't come here to sponge."

"You are a greater burden than a cadger," he said. "You deceived me, telling me you can't drink wine, yet I see you consuming it by the cupful. It's my fault: I let myself be duped by you."

He then made a binding oath never again in his life to invite a stranger to his house.

I left and was gone a few days before I found myself back at his house. He was watching the road from his window, and when he saw me he cried out to his servant, "Man the doors and the entrance! That deceitful charlatan is back. I worry he'll besiege us or climb into the house!" 12.4

When I saw him, I tried to greet him politely but he turned away and ignored me, so I recited:

> "It is as if no pilgrim ever visited al-Ḥajūn or Ṣafā,
>   or whiled away the evening in Mecca."

His retort to this was:

> "We were its people but the fates destroyed us—
>   us and itinerant doctors."

He cut me dead and shuttered the window. I left, and it was the last I ever saw of him.

We have accomplished what we promised to do insofar as our talents and power of expression allowed. We contrived that humor should be the path to seriousness—humankind hovers between emotion and intellect. We used pseudonyms for real people, letting readers infer their identity from their words. We have been quite prolix: when our power of expression finds a stage it has a tendency to ramble on, and our thoughts develop when a generous occasion lends itself. Had we wished to, we could have expatiated even further and run the risk of boring our reader. 13.1

We hope what we have produced in prose and verse has the power to please. We ask God to take us from this fleeting world full of troubles into His holy presence—to the goal the soul seeks, the home of true intimacy, where no desire is stinted and no beloved is relinquished—where ease and a peaceful and contented heart will thrive. He hears and responds.

Notes

1 Third sovereign of the Marwanid dynasty, which ruled over the area of Diyār Bakr from their capital at Mayyāfāriqīn—the location of the events of *The Doctors' Dinner Party*. He reigned 401–53/1011–61.

2 A true physician was considered also to be a philosopher.

3 The word used here, *fātiḥah*, is the name given to the opening surah of the Qur'an, endowing a certain solemnity to the text.

4 Economic stagnation is implied. The theme of earning a livelihood recurs throughout the text.

5 On both feast days and Fridays, when people were off from work, the city would have been crowded.

6 Literally Gamma Leonis, a binary star system that forms part of the constellation of Leo where the forehead would be; it is exceptionally luminescent.

7 Literally the 'Days' and the 'Nights,' used to convey the idea of death-dealing fate and time.

8 This spelling is consistent with the derivation from Sanskrit proposed by Kahl, "A Note on 'Arabic' *r/zāmhrān*," 578.

9 Possibly a reference to using astrological charts to select propitious days for administering medicine.

10 According to 'Izzat 'Umar, *Da'wah*, 65n9, these verses are probably by Ibn Buṭlān.

11 The concept of *taqdīr* with relation to food is the subject of a section of Ibn 'Abd Rabbih, *al-'Iqd al-farīd*, 6:310–11. The opposition of *taqdīr al-ṭa'ām* and *taqdīr al-ṣiyām* occurs in Ibn al-'Arabī, *Aḥkām al-Qur'ān*, 2:185 §19 (Q Mā'idah 5:95).

12 Also attributed to Pythagoras and Heraclitus.

13 The rebellion that brought the Marwanids to power after the Hamdanids. Ibn al-Athradī, *Réponses aux questions posées par Ibn Buṭlān dans Le banquet des médecins,* has a different, almost certainly incorrect, historical take.

14 A line famous in the lore about the celebrated pre-Islamic poet Imru' al-Qays's vengeance for his father's murder.

15 Only three of the medical natures are in fact identified.

16 All the verbs that occur in the Arabic Form II in the singing portions of the text have a technical usage, usually referring to the length of the lines sung or whether they are sung in measured tones or not. For references, consult Sawa, *Musical and Socio-Cultural Anecdotes from Kitāb al-Aghānī*, 10a2 (*hazaj*), 28f (*hazaj*), 30g (*basīṭ*).

17 For the best guide in English to the question-and-answer sessions in this and the next four parts, see Martin Levey, 'Some Eleventh Century Medical Questions Posed by Ibn Buṭlān and Later Answered by Ibn Ithirdī.' An edition and translation of the work exists: Ibn al-Athradī, *Réponses aux questions posées par Ibn Buṭlān dans Le banquet des médecins*.

18 In the Arabic this reads literally "O blessed locks!" The reference is to a group of stars or comets collectively referred to as "the locks" (*al-nawāṣī*). See Savage-Smith and Rapoport, *An Eleventh-Century Egyptian Guide to the Universe: The Book of Curiosities*, 383.

19 Qays and Lubnā, Majnūn and Laylā, and Jamīl and Buthaynah are lovers whose separation is celebrated in early Islamic verse and prose.

20 A rare reference to Christianity in the text. Perhaps some of those assembled are Christians.

21 In legend, the last vulture of Luqmān to die, signaling the death of the sage himself.

22 Cf. Q Baqarah 2:261.

23 A celebrated Umayyad princess.

24 The pairing of the names is ironic, as Abū l-Wafā' means trustworthy, and "Jārūf" means "greedy, boorish."

25 ʿAbd Allāh ibn Hilāl was a skilled sorcerer.

26 A reference to the Brethren of Purity, a group of theosophists who wrote their philosophical epistles more or less contemporaneously with Ibn Buṭlān's life.

Glossary

al-ʿAbbās ibn al-Aḥnaf (d. after 193/808) a poet active in the court of Hārūn al-Rashīd at Baghdad, best known for his highly stylized amatory verse.

Abū ʿAlī Naẓīf [Ibn Yumn al-Qass] (d. late fourth/tenth c.) a Christian preacher, he was personal physician to the Buyid regent ʿAḍud al-Dawlah (r. 372–88/983–98) and employed at the ʿAḍudī hospital. He was a translator from Greek into Arabic, and his translation of the tenth book of Euclid's *Elements* survives.

ʿAbd Allāh ibn Hilāl (fl. first half of second/eighth c.) a sorcerer active in Kufa whose alleged powers garnered him the reputation as either the friend or son-in-law of the Devil.

Abū l-Ḥusayn Ibn Naffākh (fl. fourth/tenth c.) a surgeon in the ʿAḍudī hospital of Baghdad and a contemporary of Ibn Buṭlān.

Abū Nuwās (d. 198/813 or 200/815) a poet active in the early Abbasid court at Baghdad. Notwithstanding his command of a variety of poetic genres, he is famous for being the popularizer of the wine song.

Abū l-Wafāʾ 'the geometer' (al-muhandis) Muḥammad ibn Muḥammad al-Būzjānī (d. 387/997 or 388/998), a mathematician and astronomer, active in the Buyid courts of Baghdad and Kirmān. He published popular textbooks on secretarial arithmetic, algebra, and magic squares, and proposed solutions to geometry problems first posed in Antiquity.

Aḥmad ibn Ḥanbal (d. 241/855) a famous and popular scholar of Hadith, and eponym of one of the four Sunni legal rites.

Aḥmad ibn Marwān Abū Naṣr Naṣr al-Dawlah (r. 401–53/1011–61), the third sovereign of the Kurdish Marwanid dynasty based in Mayyāfāriqīn. His court was renowned for its splendor, cultural refinement, and good relations with the Byzantines.

Aḥmad ibn Qurābah (d. 339/950) a notable of Baghdad who evaded a summons from the caliph al-Qāhir (r. 320–22/932–34) in 321/933.

ʿAmr ibn Maʿdīkarib (d. 21/642) a poet and itinerant warrior who was active both before and after the advent of Islam in Yemen, the Hijaz, and Syria.

the Ancients (al-qudamāʾ) physicians from the Hellenistic medical tradition, such as Hippocrates and Galen, whose works were translated into Arabic from Greek, Syriac, and Middle Persian in the third/ninth century.

antidote see theriac.

Bidʿah 'the elder' (d. ca. 302/915) a singer active in the Abbasid court at Baghdad.

black bile (sawdāʾ) one of the four humors combining cold and dry complexions; the counterpart of the season autumn and the element earth.

blood (dam) one of the four humors combining hot and moist complexions; the counterpart of the season spring and the element air.

bloodletting (fiṣād; faṣd) a method, distinct from cupping and the application of bloodsucking leeches, which, according to the Galenic theory of humors, relieved diseases believed to be caused by heat. Successful bloodletting, or venesection, depended on locating a precise point on the vein associated with the ailment.

broth (tharīdah; pl. tharāʾid) a simple dish often mentioned as a banquet food. The grammarian Quṭrub (d. 206/821) identifies it with the diet of ascetics, and the geographer al-Muqadassī (d. ca. 380/990) as a staple of recluses.

Bunān (d. ca. fourth/tenth c.) the archetypical *ṭufaylī*, or 'sponger,' whose appetite was matched only by his wit.

diet (ḥimyah) a course of treatment specifying limiting the intake of food, frequently associated with the non-Galenic traditions of early Arabic medicine. Ibn Buṭlān's predecessor, Muḥammad ibn Zakariyyāʾ al-Rāzī (d. 313/925), wrote a treatise condemning its excessive application.

Dioscorides (d. ca. AD 90) a Hellenistic naturalist whose famous pharmacopeia, the encyclopedic *De Materia Medica*, exerted tremendous influence on the pharmacological practices of Late Antique, Islamic, and European societies.

fālūdhaj a cake made with clarified butter, wheat, and honey. It was a delicacy praised and scorned alike owing to its Persian origin.

Galen (d. AD 216) Hellenistic physician whose theories influenced nearly every field of Arabic medical science, and to a lesser extent philosophy. The most important of his works were canonized as 'the sixteen books,' on which Ibn Buṭlān's nemesis ʿAlī ibn Riḍwān (d. 453/1068) wrote several commentaries.

al-Ḥajūn and al-Ṣafā two geographical prominences in Mecca, between which lies the grand mosque. The former is now occupied by the cemetery of al-Muʿalāt, in which members of the immediate family of the Prophet Muḥammad and other prominent Muslims are buried. The latter forms one terminus, along with al-Marwah, of the ritual journey (*saʿy*) performed during the hajj.

hazaj a musical mode.

humors (khilṭ, pl. akhlāṭ) bodily fluids responsible for processing nutrients; each humor is associated with a combination of complexions (heat, cold, moisture, and dryness), an element (fire, water, air, and earth), and a meteorological season. Hippocrates first developed the axioms of humoral pathology, later codified in the writings of Galen. In this system, illness is thought to be the result of an imbalance of the humors, and the role of the physician is to restore them to equilibrium.

Hippocrates (d. 379 BC) a Hellenistic physician, regarded in the Arabic tradition as 'the father of medicine' and 'the true physician.' Among the works that formed the Arabic *Corpus Hippocraticum*, four became especially prominent: the *Aphorisms* (*al-Fuṣūl al-Buqrāṭiyyah*); *Airs, Waters, and Places* (*Kitāb al-Ahwiyah wa-l-miyāh wa-l-masākin*); *Prognosis* (*Kitāb Taqdimat al-maʿrifah*); and *Regimen in Acute Diseases* (*Kitāb Tadbīr al-amrāḍ al-ḥāddah* or *Kitāb Māʾ al-shaʿīr*).

Ibn ʿAbdān (fl. fourth/tenth c.) an otherwise obscure physician, probably active in Baghdad, known to the litterateur Abū Ḥayyān al-Tawḥīdī.

Ibn Baks Ibrāhīm ibn Muḥammad (d. 394/1004), a blind physician and translator, active in the ʿAḍudī hospital at Baghdad, who wrote a medical compendium for the students of the hospital.

Ibn Ghassān (d. fourth/tenth c.) a poet and part-time physician from Basra whose lack of success in attracting patronage eventually drove him to drown himself in the Tigris.

Ibn Khammār Abū l-Khayr al-Ḥasan ibn Suwār (d. after 407/1017), a surgeon active at the ʿAḍudī hospital at Baghdad. He translated philosophical works from Syriac and instructed Ibn Buṭlān's teacher, Ibn al-Ṭayyib (d. 435/1043), in Aristotelian logic.

Ibn al-Muʿtazz Abū l-ʿAbbās ʿAbd Allāh (d. 296/908), a poet and literary critic, and son of the caliph al-Muʿtazz (r. 252–55/866–70).

Ibn Surayj ʿUbayd (d. ca. 108/726), a Meccan singer, composer, and performer active in the Umayyad court at Damascus, where he associated with Maʿbad ibn Wahb. Famous for his lamentations, he also composed a widely circulated list of the qualities of the outstanding singer (*al-muṣīb al-muḥsin*).

Isḥāq ibn Ḥunayn (d. 298/910) an Arab Christian physician and a leading translator of Antique sciences from Greek and Syriac sources into Arabic. His father, Ḥunayn ibn Isḥāq (d. 260/873–74), was also a physician, and was the most prominent such translator. Like his father, Isḥāq was physician to the caliphs.

Israel the Oculist perhaps ʿĪsā ibn ʿAlī al-Ṭabīb (fl. third/ninth c.), who served the caliph al-Muʿtamid (r. 256–79/870–92).

jaundice see yellow bile.

Jibrīl ibn Bukhtīshūʿ (d. 213/828) a member of a prominent Persian family of Christian doctors, active in Baghdad. He served as the personal physician of the Abbasid caliphs Hārūn al-Rashīd (r. 170–93/786–809), al-Amīn (r. 193–98/809–13), and al-Maʾmūn (r. 198–218/813–33).

Kalīlah and Dimnah A collection of fables originally composed in Sanskrit and translated from Middle Persian into Arabic by the early Abbasid secretary Ibn al-Muqaffaʿ (d. ca. 139/756).

khalanj a species of tree with exceptionally dark wood originating in the Chāch (or Chāj) region of Transoxania.

Maʿbad ibn Wahb (d. before 130/748) a singer and composer active in the Umayyad court at Damascus, where he was the companion of Ibn Surayj. He was renowned for his unparalleled singing voice and exceptionally difficult compositions.

maḍīrah a type of stew featuring meat cooked in sour milk.

al-Maʾmūn (r. 198–218/813–33) the seventh Abbasid caliph, a prominent patron of poetry, science, and translation, who was both a soldier and an intellectual.

Mayyāfāriqīn ancient Martyropolis (modern Silvan, in Turkey), the largest city in the Diyār Bakr administrative region and site of a large hospital. The city repeatedly fell under Byzantine control during the fourth/tenth century, but in Ibn Buṭlān's time it was ruled by Aḥmad ibn Marwān.

melancholy see black bile.

Munkar and Nakīr two angels who test the faith of the dead in their graves and administer punishment to those found wanting.

al-Mutanabbī Abū l-Ṭayyib Aḥmad ibn al-Ḥusayn (d. 354/965), a celebrated poet and, in his early days, a quasi-prophetic itinerant warrior active in Iraq, Egypt, and Syria.

al-Mutawakkil (r. 232–47/847–61) the tenth Abbasid caliph, who established a new capital at Sāmarrāʾ, a little north of Baghdad. He was a primary patron of the medical translations produced by Ḥunayn ibn Isḥāq (d. 260/873) and his circle, and the dedicatee of a medical treatise by ʿAlī ibn Sahl Rabban al-Ṭabarī (d. ca. 246/860).

Nowruz a popular Persian festival, celebrated at the vernal equinox and the summer solstice in Persia and Iraq.

phlegm (balgham) one of the four humors, combining cold and moist complexions; the counterpart of the season winter and the element water.

Pythagoras (fl. sixth c. BC) a Greek philosopher. In the Arabic tradition, he is believed to have inaugurated the study of science, music, and alchemy. His treatise *Golden Verses* (*al-Aqwāl al-dhahabiyyah*) was said to have influenced Galen, and was the subject of commentaries authored by Ibn Buṭlān's teacher Ibn al-Ṭayyib, as well as his nemesis ʿAlī ibn Riḍwān.

Qirwāsh ibn al-Muqallad (r. 391–441/1002–50, d. 444/1052) the third sovereign of the Musayyab branch of the ʿUqaylī dynasty, who served as the regent of the northern Mesopotamian cities of Mosul and al-Madā'in.

ramal a musical mode.

Shājī (d. fourth/tenth c.) a singer in the court of al-Muʿtaḍid (r. 285–89/892–902), and the favorite consort of the vizier ʿUbayd Allāh ibn ʿAbd Allāh ibn Ṭāhir (d. 300/913–14).

Socrates (d. 399 BC) the Greek philosopher, viewed in the Arabic tradition as a moral sage and uncompromising monotheist.

Surayrah al-Rā'iqiyyah (d. ca. 302/915) a famous singer in the Abbasid courts of Sāmarrā' and Baghdad.

temple medicine (ṭibb al-hayākil) a therapeutic tradition in which a patient undertook ritualized sleep in the hope of receiving a cure or indications for a course of treatment in a dream. The most frequently undertaken treatments included bathing, purging, and adhering to a specific diet. A description of the types of incense used in temple medicine therapies and their effects forms the last chapter of Ibn Buṭlān's medical guide for monks.

theriac (tiryāq) a complex electuary, considered a universal antidote. In the Arabic tradition prior to Ibn Buṭlān, numerous physicians proposed recipes following the purported formulation of Galen.

ʿUmārah ibn Ḥamzah (fl. late second/eighth c.) a secretary of the early Abbasid state, renowned for his eloquence, generosity, and vanity, the last of which became proverbial.

yellow bile, gall (ṣafrā') one of the four humors, combining hot and dry complexions; counterpart of the season spring and the element fire.

Zaʿfarān Monastery a remote monastery in the Ṭūr ʿĀbidīn area, located approximately three and a half miles (six kilometers) east of Mardin (in modern-day Turkey). In the fourth/tenth century it was best known for its idyllic vineyards. It later housed an important manuscript library, and from the sixth/twelfth century served as the seat of the Patriarch of Antioch, the head of the Syrian Orthodox Church.

Bibliography

Athenaeus. *The Learned Banqueters*. Vol. 1, bks. 1–3, edited and translated by S. Douglas Olson. Loeb Classical Library 106e. Cambridge, MA: Harvard University Press, 2007.

Baker, Colin F. "A Note on an Arabic Fragment of Ibn Buṭlān's 'The Physicians' Dinner Party' from the Cairo Geniza." *Journal of the Royal Asiatic Society*, third series, 3, no. 2 (1993): 207–13.

Beaumont, Daniel. "A Mighty and Never Ending Affair: Comic Anecdote and Story in Medieval Arabic Literature." *Journal of Arabic Literature* 24, no. 2 (1993): 139–59.

Conrad, Lawrence. "Ibn Butlān in *Bilād al-Shām*: The Career of a Travelling Christian Physician." In *Syrian Christians under Islam: The First Thousand Years*, edited by David Thomas, 131–57. Leiden, Netherlands: Brill, 2001.

Contadini, Anna. *A World of Beasts: A Thirteenth-Century Illustrated Book on Animals (the Kitāb Naʿt al-Ḥayawān) in the Ibn Buḫtīshūʿ Tradition*. Leiden, Netherlands: Brill, 2012.

Faultless, Julian. "Ibn al-Ṭayyib." In *Christian–Muslim Relations: A Bibliographical History*, vol. 2 (900–1050), edited by David Thomas and Alex Mallett, 667–97. Leiden, Netherlands: Brill, 2010.

Fenton, Paul. *Ršiymat kitbey-yad bʿarbiyt-yhwdiyt bLeniyngrad: Ršiymah ʾarʿiyt šel kitbey-yad bʿarbiyt-yhwdiyt bʾwspey Piyrqwbiyṣ* [*A Handlist of Judeo-Arabic Manuscripts in Leningrad: A Tentative Handlist of Judeo-Arabic Manuscripts of the Firkovic Collections*]. Jerusalem: Mekhon Ben Tzvi, 1991.

Goitein, S. D. F. "The Medical Profession." In *A Mediterranean Society: The Jewish Communities of the Arab World as Portrayed in the Documents of the Cairo Geniza*, vol. 2, 240–60. Berkeley: University of California Press, 1971.

Graf, G., ed. and trans. "Die Eucharistielehre des Nestorianers Al-Muḫṭār ibn Buṭlan (11. Jahrhunderds)." *Oriens christianus*, series 3, 13 (1938): 44–70, 175–91.

Ibn ʿAbd Rabbih, Aḥmad ibn Muḥammad. *Al-ʿIqd al-farīd*. Edited by Aḥmad Amīn, Ibrāhīm al-Abyārī, and ʿAbd al-Salām Hārawī. Cairo: Lajnat al-Taʾlīf wa-l-Tarjamah wa-l-Nashr, 1965.

Ibn Abī Uṣaybiʿah, Abū l-ʿAbbās Aḥmad. *ʿUyūn al-anbāʾ fī ṭabaqāt al-aṭibbāʾ* (= *A Literary History of Medicine: The Best Accounts of the Classes of Physicians*). Edited and translated by Emilie Savage-Smith, Simon Swain, and Geert Jan van Gelder. Brill Online, 2020. DOI:10.1163/37704_0668IbnAbiUsaibia.Tabaqatalatibba.lhom-ed-ara1.

Ibn al-ʿArabī, Abū Bakr. *Aḥkām al-Qurʾān*. Edited by Muḥammad ʿAbd al-Qādir ʿAṭā. Beirut: Dār al-Kutub al-ʿIlmiyyah, 2003.

Ibn al-Athradī, ʿAlī ibn Hibat Allāh. *Réponses aux questions posées par Ibn Buṭlān dans Le banquet des médecins*. Edited and translated by Joseph Dagher and Gérard Troupeau. Paris: Paul Geunther, 2011.

Ibn Buṭlān, Abū l-Ḥasan Mukhṭār (= Yūwānis) ibn al-Ḥasan ibn Ḥamdūn ibn Saʿdūn. *Daʿwat al-aṭibbāʾ*, Biblioteca Ambrosiana, 125 A *antico fondo* Inf. (S.P.67 bis). Biblioteca Ambrosiana Collection, Hesburgh Libraries, University of Notre Dame. Microfilm.

———. *Daʿwat al-aṭibbāʾ*, Wellcome Institute, MS Arabic 471. https://wellcomecollection.org/works/edtk8ecb.

———. *Das Ärtzbankett, Eine Ärtzsatire*. Translated by Felix Klein-Franke. Stuttgart, Germany: Hippokrates Verlag, 1984.

———. *Un banquet de médecins au temps de l'Émir Nasr El-Dawla Ibn Marwan (Daâwat el-Atibba d'Ibn Batlane)*. Translated by Mahmoud Sedky Bey. Cairo: Imprimerie Misr, 1928.

———. *Le banquet des médecins: Une maqāma médicale du XIe siècle*. Translated by Joseph Dagher and Gérard Troupeau. Paris: Paul Geunther, 2007.

———. *Daʿwat al-aṭibbāʾ*. Edited by Bishārah Zalzal. Alexandria, Egypt: Al-Maṭbaʿah al-Khidīwiyyah, 1901.

———. *Daʿwat al-aṭibbāʾ*. Edited by Iskandar al-Bārūdī. In *Al-Ṭabīb* 13, no. 1 (June 1901): 27–31; 13, no. 2 (July 1901): 35–39; 13, no. 3 (August 1901): 89–93; 13, no. 4 (September 1901): 119–23; 13, no. 5 (October 1901): 151–54; 13, no. 6 (November 1901): 180–88; 13, no. 7 (December 1901): 217–18.

———. *Kitāb Daʿwat al-aṭibbāʾ*. Edited by ʿĀdil Bakrī. Baghdad: Al-Majmaʿ al-ʿIlmī al-ʿArabī al-Islāmī, 2002.

———. *Daʿwat al-aṭibbāʾ: Ṣafaḥāt min al-adab al-ṭibbī al-Islāmī*. Edited by ʿIzzat ʿUmar. Damascus: Dār al-Fikr, 2002.

———. *The Physicians' Dinner Party*. Edited by Felix Klein-Franke. Wiesbaden, Germany: Otto Harrassowitz, 1984.

Ibn Ḥajar al-ʿAsqalānī, Abū l-Faḍl Aḥmad ibn ʿAlī. *Al-Durar al-kāminah fī aʿyān al-miʾah al-thāminah*. 4 vols. Hyderabad, India: Dāʾirat al-Maʿārif al-ʿUthmāniyyah, 1349/1930.

Ibn Khallikān, Aḥmad b. Muḥammad. *Wafayāt al-aʿyān wa-anbāʾ abnāʾ al-zamān*. 8 vols. Edited by Iḥsān ʿAbbās. Beirut: Dār Ṣādir, 1972.

Ibn al-Muqaffaʿ. *Kalīlah and Dimnah: Fables of Virtue and Vice*. Edited by Michael Fishbein and translated by Michael Fishbein and James E. Montgomery. New York: New York University Press, 2022.

Kahl, Oliver. "A Note on 'Arabic' *r/zāmhrān*." *Arabica* 58, no. 6 (2011): 571–78.

Kozodoy, Maud. "The Physicians of Medieval Iberia (1100–1500)." In *The Jew in Medieval Iberia 1100–1500*, edited by Jonathan Ray, 102–38. Brighton, MA: Academic Studies Press, 2012.

Levey, Martin. "Some Eleventh Century Medical Questions Posed by Ibn Butlan and Later Answered by Ibn Ithirdi." *Bulletin of Medical History* 39, no. 6 (1965): 495–507.

Löfgren, Oscar. "Unbekannte arabische Texte in der Ambrosiana." *Orientalia Suecana* 12 (1963): 122–34.

Marzolph, Ulrich. "The Migration of Didactic Narratives across Religious Boundaries." In *Didaktisches Erzählen: Formen literarischer Belehrung in Orient und Okzident*, edited by Regula Forster and Romy Günthart, 173–88. Frankfurt: Peter Lang, 2010.

Oltean, Daniel. "From Baghdad to Antioch and Constantinople." *Byzantinische Zeitschrift* 114, no. 1 (2021): 35–76.

Orfali, Bilal W., and Maurice A. Pomerantz. "A Lost Maqāma of Badīʿ al-Zamān al-Hamadhanī." *Arabica* 60 (2013), 245–71.

Pietrobelli, Antoine, and Marie Cronier. "Arabic Galenism from Antioch to Byzantium: Ibn Buṭlān and Symeon Seth." *Mediterranea* 7 (2022): 281–315.

Pormann, Peter. "The Physician and the Other: Images of the Charlatan in Medieval Islam." *Bulletin of the History of Medicine* 79, no. 2 (2005), 189–227.

Savage-Smith, E. S., and Peter Pormann. *Medieval Islamic Medicine*. Edinburgh: Edinburgh University Press, 2007.

Savage-Smith, Emilie, and Yossef Rapoport, eds. *An Eleventh-Century Egyptian Guide to the Universe: The Book of Curiosities*. Leiden, Netherlands: Brill, 2014.

Sedky Bey, Mahmoud. *Risālah ʿan al-ṭibb fī ayyām al-ʿArab wa-qawānīn al-ṣiḥḥah ʿind al-Muslimīn*. Translated by Ḥāfiẓ Ṣidqī. Cairo: Maṭbaʿat Abī l-Hawl, 1328/1910.

Selove, Emily. *The Ḥikāyat Abī al-Qāsim: A Literary Banquet*. Edinburgh: Edinburgh University Press, 2016.

Al-Sulamī, ʿAbd al-ʿAzīz. *Questions and Answers for Physicians: A Medieval Arabic Study Manual*. Edited and translated by Gary Leiser and Noury Khaledy. Leiden, Netherlands: Brill, 2004.

Szilágyi, Kristina. "Christian Books in Jewish Libraries: Fragments of Christian Arabic Writings from the Cairo Genizah." *Ginzei Qedem: Geniza Research Annual* 2 (2006): 107–62.

Al-Tawḥīdī, Abū Ḥayyān ʿAlī ibn Muḥammad. *Kitāb al-Imtāʿ wa-l-muʾānasah*. 3 vols. printed in one. Edited by Aḥmad Amīn and Aḥmad Zayn. Cairo: Maṭbaʿat Lajnat al-Taʾlīf wa-l-Tarjamah wa-l-Nashr, 1939–44.

Al-Tawḥīdī, Abū Ḥayyān ʿAlī ibn Muḥammad. "Risālat al-ḥayāh." In *Thalāth rasāʾil li-Abī Ḥayyān al-Tawḥīdī*, edited by Ibrāhīm Kaylānī, 51–80. Damacus: Institute Français de Damas, 1951.

Thomas, David, and John Chesworth, eds. *Christian-Muslim Relations Online*, II. Brill Online. 2017–.

Van Gelder, Geert Jan. *God's Banquet: Food in Classical Arabic Literature.* New York: Columbia University Press, 2000 = *Of Dishes and Discourse: Classical Arabic Literary Representations of Food*. London: Routledge, 2000.

Ziriklī, Khayr al-Dīn. *Al-Aʿlām: Qāmūs tarājim li-ashhar al-rijāl wa-l-nisāʾ min al-ʿArab wa-l-mustaʿribīn wa-l-mustashriqīn.* 8 vols. Reprint, Beirut: Dār al-ʿIlm li-l-Milāyīn, 1999 [1373–90/1954–70].

Further Reading

Humor and Rogues in *Adab* Literature

The *adab* tradition is typified by a judicious mixture of humorous and edifying discourse. Jocularity, knavery, and the combination of the two have inspired a variety of notable monographs and edited volumes, including:

Abu l-Qāsim al-Baghdādī (attr.). *The Portrait of Abū l-Qāsim al-Baghdādī al-Tamīmī*. Edited and translated by Emily Selove and Geert Jan van Gelder. London: Gibb Memorial Trust, 2021.

Bosworth, Clifford E. *The Mediaeval Islamic Underworld: The Banū Sāsān in Arabic Society and Literature*. 2 vols. Leiden, Netherlands: Brill, 1976.

Al-Ḥarīrī, Abū Muḥammad al-Qāsim ibn ʿAlī. *Impostures* (= *al-Maqāmāt*). Edited and translated by Michael Cooperson. New York: New York University Press, 2020.

Al-Jawbarī, Jamāl al-Dīn ʿAbd al-Raḥīm. *The Book of Charlatans* (= *Kitāb al-Mukhtār fī kashf al-asrār*). Edited by Manuela Dengler and translated by Humphrey Davies. New York: New York University Press, 2020.

Al-Khaṭīb al-Baghdādī, Abū Bakr Muḥammad. *Selections from The Art of Party-Crashing in Medieval Iraq*. Translated by Emily Selove. Syracuse. NY: Syracuse University Press, 2012.

Lerner, Amir. *The Juʿaydiyya Cycle: Witty Beggars' Stories from the Montague Manuscript—A Late Augmented Arabian Nights; A Study and a Critical Edition*. Dortmund, Germany: Verlag für Orientkunde, 2014.

Malti-Douglas, Fedwa. *Structures of Avarice: The Buḫalāʾ in Medieval Arabic Literature*. Leiden, Netherlands: Brill, 1985.

Petry, Carl. *The Criminal Underworld in a Medieval Islamic Society: Narratives from Cairo and Damascus under the Mamluks*. Chicago: Middle East Documentation Center, 2012.

Rosenthal, Franz. *Humor in Early Islam*. 2nd edition. Leiden, Netherlands: Brill, 2011.

Selove, Emily. *The Ḥikāyāt Abī al-Qāsim: A Literary Banquet*. Edinburgh: Edinburgh University Press, 2016.

Khawam, René R., trans. *The Subtle Ruse: The Book of Arabic Wisdom and Guile*. London: East-West Publications, 1980.

Tamer, Georges, ed. *Humor in der arabischen Kultur / Humor in Arabic Culture*. Berlin: Walter de Gruyter, 2009.

Food, Wine, Banquets

Works that take the culinary arts not only as a point of departure for the study of cultural expression, but also as an integral part of medical theory, legal discourse, and logistics networks include:

Dmitriev, Kirill, Julia Hauser, and Bilal Orfali, eds. *Insatiable Appetite: Food as Cultural Signifier in the Middle East and Beyond*. Leiden, Netherlands: Brill, 2019.

Dmitriev, Kirill, and Christine van Ruymbeke, eds. *"Passed around by a Crescent": Wine Poetry in the Literary Traditions of the Islamic World*. Beirut: Orient-Institut and Würzburg: Ergon-Verlag, 2022.

Al-Ghazālī, Abū Ḥāmid Muḥammad. *Al-Ghazālī on the Manners Relating to Eating: Book XI of the Revival of the Religious Sciences* (= *Kitāb ādāb al-akl, Iḥyā ʿulūm al-dīn*). Cambridge, UK: Islamic Texts Society, 2000.

Ibn Sayyār al-Warrāq, al-Muẓaffar ibn Naṣr. *Annals of the Caliphs' Kitchens: Ibn Sayyār al-Warrāq's Tenth-Century Baghdadi Cookbook*. Translated by Nawal Nasrallah. Leiden, Netherlands: Brill, 2007.

Kennedy, Philip. *Abu Nuwas: A Genius of Poetry*. Oxford: Oneworld, 2005.

Lewicka, Paulina. *Food and Foodways of Medieval Cairenes: Aspects of Life in an Islamic Metropolis of the Eastern Mediterranean*. Leiden, Netherlands: Brill, 2011.

Perry, Charles, ed. and trans. *Scents and Flavors: A Syrian Cookbook*. New York: New York University Press, 2017.

Rowell, Alex. *Vintage Humour: The Islamic Wine Poetry of Abu Nuwas*. London: Hurst, 2017.

Waines, David, ed. *Food, Culture and Health in Pre-Modern Islamic Societies*. Leiden, Netherlands: Brill, 2011.

Medicine

Accessible monographs on the intellectual and social dimensions of contemporary medicine include:

Amar, Zohar, and Efraim Levy. *Arabian Drugs in Medieval Mediterranean Medicine*. Edinburgh: Edinburgh University Press, 2017.

Chipman, Leigh. *The World of Pharmacy and Pharmacists in Mamlūk Cairo*. Leiden, Netherlands: Brill, 2010.

Graziani, Joseph Salvatore. *Arabic Medicine in the Eleventh Century as Represented in the Works of Ibn Jazlah*. Karachi, Pakistan: Hamdard Academy, 1980.

Hamarneh, Sami Khalaf. *Directory of Historians of Arabic-Islamic Science*. Aleppo, Syria: Maʿhad al-Turāth al-ʿIlmī al-ʿArabī, 1979.

Meyerhoff, Max. *Studies in Medieval Arabic Medicine: Theory and Practice*. Edited by Penelope Johnstone. London: Variorum, 1984.

Morrow, John Andrew. *Encyclopedia of Islamic Herbal Medicine*. London: MacFarland, 2011.

Pormann, Peter E. *1001 Cures: Contributions in Medicine and Healthcare from Muslim Civilizations*. Manchester, UK: Foundation for Science, Technology and Civilisation, 2018.

———. *The Mirror of Health: Discovering Medicine in the Golden Age of Islam*. London: Royal College of Physicians of London, 2013.

Pormann, Peter E., and Emilie Savage-Smith. *Medieval Islamic Medicine*. Edinburgh: Edinburgh University Press, 2007.

Ragab, Ahmed. *The Medieval Islamic Hospital: Medicine, Religion, and Charity*. Cambridge: Cambridge University Press, 2015.

———. *Piety and Patienthood in Medieval Islam*. Cambridge: Cambridge University Press, 2018.

Ullmann, Manfred. *Islamic Medicine*. Edinburgh: Edinburgh University Press, 1978.

Index of Materia Medica

Scientific name	English	Arabic
Anabasis aphylla	alkali salt	أشنان
Astragalus sarcocolla	sarcocolla balsam	أنْزَرُوت
Berberis vulgaris	barberry	أمير باريس
Terminalia chebula	black myrobalan	اهْلِيلَج أسود
Menispermum spp.	moonseed	بذور القمريّة
—	lizard dung	بعر الضبّ
Citrullus spp.	watermelon	بطّيخ
Quercus spp.	acorn	بلّوط
Alhagi maurorum	camelthorn	ترنجبين أبيض
—	tutty	التوتياء الحَشْريّ
Piper cubea	cubeb	حبّ العروس
Triticum spelta L.	wheat (spelt)	حنطة
Citrullus colocynthus	colocynth	حنظل
—	cow's dung	خثي البقر
—	dog's dung	خراء الكلب
Acorus calamus	sweet flag (incense)	دخنة
—	"Mother Mary's" incense	دخنة مريم
—	analgesic cream	دهن العافية
Foeniculum vulgare	fennel	رازْيانّج
Rheum ribes	rhubarb	راوند
Phoenix dactylifera spp.	date	رُطَب
—	wolf's dung	زبل الذئب
Cyperus spp.	sedge	سُعد
—	oxymel	سِكَنْجبِين

Scientific name	English	Arabic
—	dental paste	سَنون
Sorbus aria	whitebeam	الغُبَيراء الصينيّ
—	zinc sulphate lotion	غسول أحمر
Mentha pulegium	wild pennyroyal	فُوتَنْك
Cinammomum camphora	camphor	كافور
Mandragora officinarum	mandrake	لفّاح
—	whey	ماء الجبن
—	barley water	ماء الشعير
Prunus armeniaca	apricot	مشمش
—	*zāmaharān* electuary	معجون الزامَهران
Dorema ammoniacum	sal ammoniac	نوشادر
Cicorium intybus	endive	هندباء

Index

camphor, §11.6
canines, §2.7, §2.14
cataracts, §1.12, §2.12, §5.3
catheters, §2.12
cavalry, §9.3
cemeteries, §1.9, §1.24
chancery officials, §1.9
charity, §1.6, §2.11, §8.5
charlatans, xxx, xxxv, §§6.4–6, §7.3, §§10.14–15, §12.4
chestnuts, §11.6
chewing, xxix, §2.2, §2.7, §2.13
chicory, §2.2
chills, §10.19
cholera, §2.8
Christianity: Nestorianism, xxi, xxv, xxxvii; split between Rome and Byzantium, xxiv
Cicero, xxxviii
circumcisions, §1.6
cleaning/cleansing/washing, §1.10, §2.3, §2.12, §2.13, §7.3, §10.8, §10.9
cleansing. *See* cleaning/cleansing/washing
clothing, §4.3, §9.1, §9.3, §9.8, §9.9
coffin bearers, §1.8
coffins, §9.9
colic, §2.9, §2.12, §10.7, §11.6
collyrium, §6.4, §7.3
colocynth, §8.3
complexion (of skin), §9.11
complexions (associated with humors), §10.19
A Composition, in the Style of "The Doctors' Dinner Party" (*Kitāb ʿalā madhhab Daʿwat al-aṭibbāʾ*) (Ibn Muṭrān), xxxiv
concubines, §9.4
condiments, §2.2, §2.7
Conduct of the Secretaries (Ibn Qutaybah), §10.16
conjunctivitis, §2.12
Constantinople, xxiv
constellations, §9.7
constipation, §10.19, §11.7
constitution, xxiii, §2.9, §4.2, §10.3, §11.3, §11.8
contractions, §7.6
convalescence, §2.5, §2.14, §§6.5–6, §10.13
corps washers, §1.10, §6.5
corpses, §1.9
cosmetics, §7.3
cost of living, §2.14
coughing, §2.2, §10.17, §10.18
cow's dung, §10.8
cravings, §2.4, §2.12
Crucifixion, §11.9
crying, §9.7, §10.9, §10.17, §11.7, §11.11
cubeb, §7.3
cupping, §§7.4–5

dates, §2.10, §10.17
death, §1.6, §6.5, §10.6, §§11.2–5
defecation, §10.6
Deipnosophists, xxx
delirium, §10.6
dental pastes, §9.9
dentists, §1.9, §10.3
desserts, §§2.10–12, §12.2
al-Dhahabī, xxvi
diarrhea, §10.7, §10.19
diastolic beat, §10.17
The Dictionary of Places (*Muʿjam al-buldān*) (Yāqūt al-Ḥamawī), xxii
diet (*ḥimyah*), xxvi, xxxii, §§2.3–10, §2.14, §9.1, §11.2, §11.8

hatred, §10.9, §10.11
hazaj mode, §5.3, §6.1
health, xxxii, §1.7, §2.4, §2.11, §2.13, §3.3, §7.1, §9.1, §9.5, §10.16, §10.19, §11.4
heart beats, §9.5, §§10.16–17
hearts, §2.8, §3.2, §6.1, §7.2, §9.7, §9.10, §10.11, §11.2
hemiplegia, §2.9
hemorrhoid hooks, §2.12
henna, §8.4, §11.6
herbs, §2.7
heresy, §11.5
Hippocrates: on abstention of food, §2.5; art of, §10.19; books of, §4.4; dictum of, §6.4; on eating, §2.6; on illness's prognosis, §11.4; medicine of, xxv, §6.3; on wine, §3.2; works of, §4.4
hips, §2.12, §10.9
The History of Scientists (*Tārīkh al-ḥukamāʾ*) (Ibn al-Qifṭī), xxii
hooves, §9.1
horoscopes, §7.2
hospital rats, xxxi, §7.4
hospitality, xxvii, xxxii, §2.1
hospitals, xxii, xxii, xxiv. *See also* Aḍudī hospital
humors (*khilṭ*, pl. *akhlāṭ*), §3.4. *See also* black bile; bloodletting; Galenic system of medicine; yellow bile/gall
Ḥunayn ibn Isḥāq, xxiii, xxv, xxxiii, xxxvii–xxxviii

Ibn ʿAbdān, §§1.3–4
Ibn Abī Uṣaybiʿah, xxxiv
Ibn al-Athradī, xxxiv
Ibn Baks, §§1.3–4
Ibn Bassām al-Shantarīnī, xxxiv
Ibn Buṭlān: Aleppan antipathy towards, xxiv; becoming a monk, xxiv; biography, xxi–xxv; Ibn Riḍwān and, xxiii–xxiv; teacher of (*see* Ibn al-Ṭayyib); travels of, xxii–xxiv; works of, xxi–xxii
Ibn Ghassān, §11.4
Ibn Khallikān, xxxiv
Ibn Khammār, §§1.3–4
Ibn al-Muʿtazz, §8.1
Ibn Muṭrān, xxxiv
Ibn al-Qifṭī, xxii, xxviii
Ibn Qutaybah, §10.16
Ibn Riḍwān, xxiii–xxiv
Ibn Sīnā, xxv–xxvi
Ibn Surayj, §4.4
Ibn Suwār, §§1.3–4
Ibn Taymiyyah, xxvi
Ibn al-Ṭayyib, xxi–xxii, xxiii, xxxiv
Ibn Zabārah, xxxiv
ice, §11.6
ignoramus, §10.13, §10.18
ignorance: of charlatans, §§6.3–4; Galen on, §10.14; life expectancy and, §11.4; of young man, §§4.3–4, §5.3, §6.6, §7.7, §8.3
illnesses: food and, §1.13, §§2.4–5, §2.9; occurring in autumn, §1.7. *See also* diseases; eye ailments; stomach/stomach ailments
immortality, §11.5
immunity, §1.7
impurities, §2.9, §7.6
Imruʾ al-Qays, 80n14
inappetence, §1.13
incense, §8.4
incisions, §7.4, §7.6
incisors, §2.7

al-Qāsim ibn ʿUbaydullah, §9.5
Qays and Lubnā, §4.4, 80n19
Qirwāsh ibn al-Muqallad, §1.6
quack medicine, §0.1, §1.12, §9.6
Qurʾan, §1.4, §7.3

rain, §1.6, §6.1, §11.9
ramal mode, §5.3
reconciliation, §§10.9–10
The Repository of the Virtues of the Inhabitants of the Iberian Peninsula (*al-Dhakhīrah fī maḥāsin ahl al-Jazīrah*) (Ibn Bassām al-Shantarīnī), xxxiv
reputation, §1.5, §11.11
respiration, §10.17
rhubarb, §2.2
rice pudding, §2.10
*risālah*s (epistles), xxix
romantic fiction, §4.4
rosewater, §8.4

al-Ṣābiʾ, Ghars al-Niʿmah, xxii
al-Ṣābiʾ, Hilāl, xxii
al-Ṣafā, §12.4
al-Ṣafadī, xxxvii
sal ammoniac, §7.3, §8.4
saliva, §10.6
salts, §2.13, §10.8
salty foods, §2 .2, §2.7
sarcocolla balsam, §1.12
Savage-Smith, Emilie, xxxviii
saws, §2.12
scabies, §2.12
scabs, §10.9
scales, §8.4, §10.4
scalpel receptacles, §2.12
scalpels, §3.4, §§7.5–7, §9.5, §10.11, §11.11
scars, §6.3, §10.11
sciatic nerve, §2.12
science, §1.4, §3.3, §6.3, §9.6, §10.12, §10.19, §11.5
scoops, §2.12
Scorpio, §9.11
scrapers, §2.12
sedges, §10.8
semen, §4.3
sensum de sensu (meaning for meaning) translation technique, xxxviii
servant boy: bringing of food and wine by, xxvi, §2.1, §§3.1–3; cursing of, §2.2; eating of food by, xxvii, §§11.1–2; presenting alkali salts by, §2.13; summoned to close doors, §12.4; taking away of food by, §§2.9–10, §2.12
servants, §1.6, §2.7, §7.2, §9.11, §10.4
Shājī (singer), §7.1
shame, §9.1, §9.9, §10.11, §11.5
Shaʿthā, §7.3, §8.4
Sheba, §11.6
shoulder splints, §2.12
shrouds, §1.9, §9.9
sieves, §8.4
sighing, §6.1, §6.5, §10.15, §10.17
silkworms, xxviii, §2.3
sinews, §6.2
singing of songs: of al-ʿAbbās ibn al-Aḥnaf, §11.10; about sickness, §11.10; by Abū Jābir, §3.4, §6.1, §7.1, §9.7, §12.1; inappropriate for the moment, §§11.8–9
sins, §2.3
skin, §3.2, §9.11, §10.19
slander, §9.1, §10.12
Slavs, §4.2
sleep, §4.3, §7.4, §10.6, §10.15, §11.7, §11.8, §12.2

snakes/vipers, §11.3
sneezing, §10.17
soaps, §7.3, §8.4
social graces, §9.2
Socrates, §2.3, §2.6
solace, §9.6, §10.11
sorcerers. *See* ʿAbd Allāh ibn Hilāl
sorrow, §10.11, §11.11
souls, §2.3, §2.7, §2.11, §2.13, §4.1, §6.4, §7.2, §9.10, §10.18, §11.11, §13.1
soups, §2.7
spheroid objects, §10.18
spindles, §2.12
spitting, §10.17
spittle, §9.1
spleen, §2.12
splints, shoulder, §2.12
spongers (*ṭufaylī*s), §2.14, §12.3
sponges, §8.3
stinginess, §2.12, §3.2
stomach/stomach ailments: appetites and, §2.14, §4.4; food's effects on, §§2.2–3, §2.7; indigestion, §2.5; reduced appetite, §1.13; of sick old man, §11.7; sinews or fibers in, §6.2; upset by wine, §2.14; of young man, xvi, xxi, §1.12, §2.5
stones, §2.14, §8.3
street sweepers, §2.3
students, medical, xxxiii, §1.4, §10.13
stylusses, §6.4
Sukaynah (hairdresser), §8.4
Sukaynah, Umayyad princess, §7.3
al-Sulamī, xxxiii
Surayrah (singer), §4.4
surgeons, xxvii, §5.4, §6.2, §6.6. *See also* Abū Sālim
surgical procedures, §6.2
al-Suyūṭī, xxvi
sweating, §§10.6–7
swindlers, §9.11. *See also* charlatans
swine, §4.2
symptoms, §10.2, §10.3
Syria, xxiv
syringes, §2.12
systolic beat, §10.17

Tacuinum Sanitatis (Ibn Buṭlān), xxi
tambourines, §1.10
tanning process, §10.8
tasting, §1.9, §2.2, §2.4, §2.8, §4.2, §8.3
teeth, xxv, §2.7, §2.10, §2.12, §6.1, §6.3, §10.9, §10.16. *See also* incisors; molars
temple medicine (*ṭibb al-hayākil*), xxvi, §1.12
theosophists, 122n26
thighs, §2.8
throats, §1.7, §2.2, §2.8
tongues, §2.2, §2.7, §2.10, §8.3, §10.11
tranquility, §10.19
translation movement, xxxvii
trotters, §2.9
*ṭufaylī*s (spongers), §2.14, §12.3
tumors, §2.12
tutty, §8.3

Ulayyah (midwife), §8.4
ulcers, §10.8
ʿUmārah ibn Ḥamzah, §1.9
urinating, §4.3, §10.6
urine, §2.8, §4.3, §6.4, §7.3, §9.1, §10.2, §10.6, §10.8, §11.7
uterus, §2.12

Van Gelder, Geert Jan, xxxi
vegetables, §2.7. *See also under specific vegetables*

vena basilica, §7.4
vena salvatella, §7.4
venesection (bloodletting), §1.6, §6.4, §§7.4–5, §7.1, §10.19
verbum de verbo (word for word) translation technique, xxxviii
veterinarians, §11.2
veterinary science, §11.5
vinegars, §2.1, §2.2, §2.8, §8.2
vipers/snakes, §11.3

washbasins, §8.4
washing. *See* cleaning/cleansing/washing
water: abundance of, §11.9; blood and, §7.4; briny, §8.6; cleaning with, §10.8; compared to wine, §3.5; drinking of, §2.7, §2.10, §10.17; eyes and, §5.1; fire and, §10.11; fresh, §9.8; iced, §2.10; liquid medicines and, §8.2; stagnant, §1.11; sweet, §8.6; writing on, §10.12. *See also* barley water; rosewater; urinating
watermelons, §11.6
weaning, §1.6
weddings/wedding parties, §1.10, §11.9
weeping. *See* crying
well-being, §2.11
wheat, §2.2
whey, §9.11
whitebeam berries, §8.3
wicked people, §12.3
wind instruments, §10.17
wine: Abū Nuwās on, §§3.4–5; Abū Sālim on, §6.1; benefits of, §10.17; drinking of, §2.14, §§3.1–2, §4.2, §5.2, §5.3, §6.1, §7.1, §8.1, §§9.7–8, §12.2, §12.13; expert pouring of, §10.18; Ibn al-Muʿtazz on, §8.1
wine cups, §9.7. *See also* goblets
wisdom, xxviii, §2.3, §8.6
wisdom teeth, §6.3
wolf's dung, §8.3, §10.8
women, pregnant, §9.11, §10.17, §11.3
wounds, §6.3, §7.7, §10.9, §10.11, §10.16

yawning, §10.17
youth, misspent, §5.3, §10.9
Yuḥannā ibn al-Biṭrīq, xxxvii

Zaʿfarān Monastery, §1.5, §1.12
zāmaharān electuary, §1.12
zinc sulfate lotions, §8.4
zinc tutty, §8.3

About the NYU Abu Dhabi Research Institute

The Library of Arabic Literature is a research center affiliated with NYU Abu Dhabi and is supported by a grant from the NYU Abu Dhabi Research Institute.

جامعة نيويورك أبوظبي
NYU ABU DHABI

The NYU Abu Dhabi Research Institute is a world-class center of cutting-edge and innovative research, scholarship, and cultural activity. It supports centers that address questions of global significance and local relevance and allows leading faculty members from across the disciplines to carry out creative scholarship and high-level research on a range of complex issues with depth, scale, and longevity that otherwise would not be possible.

From genomics and climate science to the humanities and Arabic literature, Research Institute centers make significant contributions to scholarship, scientific understanding, and artistic creativity. Centers strengthen cross-disciplinary engagement and innovation among the faculty, build critical mass in infrastructure and research talent at NYU Abu Dhabi, and have helped make the university a magnet for outstanding faculty, scholars, students, and international collaborations.

About the Translators

Philip F. Kennedy, the founding Faculty Director of the NYU Abu Dhabi Institute, is Professor of Middle Eastern and Islamic Studies and Comparative Literature at New York University, affiliate faculty member of NYU Abu Dhabi, and General Editor of the Library of Arabic Literature. Kennedy has published many writings on Arabic literature, including *Recognition in the Arabic Narrative Tradition: Discovery, Deliverance and Delusion* (2016); *Scheherazade's Children: Global Encounters with The Arabian Nights* (edited with Marina Warner, 2013); *Abu Nuwas: A Genius of Poetry* (2005); *On Fiction and Adab in Medieval Arabic Literature* (2004); and *The Wine Song in Classical Arabic Poetry: Abu Nuwas and the Literary Tradition* (1997).

Jeremy Farrell holds a Ph.D. from Emory University. His publications analyze diverse aspects of pre-modern Islamic society, including sarcastic speech acts, transgressive modes of piety, and the formation of cooperative networks.

The Library of Arabic Literature

For more details on individual titles, visit www.libraryofarabicliterature.org

Classical Arabic Literature: A Library of Arabic Literature Anthology
Selected and translated by Geert Jan van Gelder (2012)

A Treasury of Virtues: Sayings, Sermons, and Teachings of ʿAlī, by al-Qāḍī al-Quḍāʿī, with the *One Hundred Proverbs* attributed to al-Jāḥiẓ
Edited and translated by Tahera Qutbuddin (2013)

The Epistle on Legal Theory, by al-Shāfiʿī
Edited and translated by Joseph E. Lowry (2013)

Leg over Leg, by Aḥmad Fāris al-Shidyāq
Edited and translated by Humphrey Davies (4 volumes; 2013–14)

Virtues of the Imām Aḥmad ibn Ḥanbal, by Ibn al-Jawzī
Edited and translated by Michael Cooperson (2 volumes; 2013–15)

The Epistle of Forgiveness, by Abū l-ʿAlāʾ al-Maʿarrī
Edited and translated by Geert Jan van Gelder and Gregor Schoeler (2 volumes; 2013–14)

The Principles of Sufism, by ʿĀʾishah al-Bāʿūniyyah
Edited and translated by Th. Emil Homerin (2014)

The Expeditions: An Early Biography of Muḥammad, by Maʿmar ibn Rāshid
Edited and translated by Sean W. Anthony (2014)

Two Arabic Travel Books

Accounts of China and India, by Abū Zayd al-Sīrāfī

Edited and translated by Tim Mackintosh-Smith (2014)

Mission to the Volga, by Aḥmad ibn Faḍlān

Edited and translated by James Montgomery (2014)

Disagreements of the Jurists: A Manual of Islamic Legal Theory, by al-Qāḍī al-Nuʿmān

Edited and translated by Devin J. Stewart (2015)

Consorts of the Caliphs: Women and the Court of Baghdad, by Ibn al-Sāʿī

Edited by Shawkat M. Toorawa and translated by the Editors of the Library of Arabic Literature (2015)

What ʿĪsā ibn Hishām Told Us, by Muḥammad al-Muwayliḥī

Edited and translated by Roger Allen (2 volumes; 2015)

The Life and Times of Abū Tammām, by Abū Bakr Muḥammad ibn Yaḥyā al-Ṣūlī

Edited and translated by Beatrice Gruendler (2015)

The Sword of Ambition: Bureaucratic Rivalry in Medieval Egypt, by ʿUthmān ibn Ibrāhīm al-Nābulusī

Edited and translated by Luke Yarbrough (2016)

Brains Confounded by the Ode of Abū Shādūf Expounded, by Yūsuf al-Shirbīnī

Edited and translated by Humphrey Davies (2 volumes; 2016)

Light in the Heavens: Sayings of the Prophet Muḥammad, by al-Qāḍī al-Quḍāʿī

Edited and translated by Tahera Qutbuddin (2016)

Risible Rhymes, by Muḥammad ibn Maḥfūẓ al-Sanhūrī

Edited and translated by Humphrey Davies (2016)

A Hundred and One Nights

Edited and translated by Bruce Fudge (2016)

The Excellence of the Arabs, by Ibn Qutaybah
Edited by James E. Montgomery and Peter Webb
Translated by Sarah Bowen Savant and Peter Webb (2017)

Scents and Flavors: A Syrian Cookbook
Edited and translated by Charles Perry (2017)

Arabian Satire: Poetry from 18th-Century Najd, by Ḥmēdān al-Shwēʿir
Edited and translated by Marcel Kurpershoek (2017)

In Darfur: An Account of the Sultanate and Its People, by Muḥammad ibn ʿUmar al-Tūnisī
Edited and translated by Humphrey Davies (2 volumes; 2018)

War Songs, by ʿAntarah ibn Shaddād
Edited by James E. Montgomery
Translated by James E. Montgomery with Richard Sieburth (2018)

Arabian Romantic: Poems on Bedouin Life and Love, by ʿAbdallah ibn Sbayyil
Edited and translated by Marcel Kurpershoek (2018)

Dīwān ʿAntarah ibn Shaddād: A Literary-Historical Study, by James E. Montgomery (2018)

Stories of Piety and Prayer: Deliverance Follows Adversity, by al-Muḥassin ibn ʿAlī al-Tanūkhī
Edited and translated by Julia Bray (2019)

Tajrīd sayf al-himmah li-stikhrāj mā fī dhimmat al-dhimmah: A Scholarly Edition of ʿUthmān ibn Ibrāhīm al-Nābulusī's Text, by Luke Yarbrough (2019)

The Philosopher Responds: An Intellectual Correspondence from the Tenth Century, by Abū Ḥayyān al-Tawḥīdī and Abū ʿAlī Miskawayh
Edited by Bilal Orfali and Maurice A. Pomerantz
Translated by Sophia Vasalou and James E. Montgomery (2 volumes; 2019)

The Discourses: Reflections on History, Sufism, Theology, and Literature—Volume One, by al-Ḥasan al-Yūsī
Edited and translated by Justin Stearns (2020)

Impostures, by al-Ḥarīrī
Translated by Michael Cooperson (2020)

Maqāmāt Abī Zayd al-Sarūjī, by al-Ḥarīrī
Edited by Michael Cooperson (2020)

The Yoga Sutras of Patañjali, by Abū Rayḥān al-Bīrūnī
Edited and translated by Mario Kozah (2020)

The Book of Charlatans, by Jamāl al-Dīn ʿAbd al-Raḥīm al-Jawbarī
Edited by Manuela Dengler
Translated by Humphrey Davies (2020)

A Physician on the Nile: A Description of Egypt and Journal of the Famine Years, by ʿAbd al-Laṭīf al-Baghdādī
Edited and translated by Tim Mackintosh-Smith (2021)

The Book of Travels, by Ḥannā Diyāb
Edited by Johannes Stephan
Translated by Elias Muhanna (2 volumes; 2021)

Kalīlah and Dimnah: Fables of Virtue and Vice, by Ibn al-Muqaffaʿ
Edited by Michael Fishbein
Translated by Michael Fishbein and James E. Montgomery (2021)

Love, Death, Fame: Poetry and Lore from the Emirati Oral Tradition, by al-Māyidī ibn Ẓāhir
Edited and translated by Marcel Kurpershoek (2022)

The Essence of Reality: A Defense of Philosophical Sufism, by ʿAyn al-Quḍāt
Edited and translated by Mohammed Rustom (2022)

The Requirements of the Sufi Path: A Defense of the Mystical Tradition, by Ibn Khaldūn
Edited and translated by Carolyn Baugh (2022)

The Doctors' Dinner Party, by Ibn Buṭlān
Edited and translated by Philip F. Kennedy and Jeremy Farrell (2023)

Fate the Hunter: Early Arabic Hunting Poems
Edited and translated by James E. Montgomery (2023)

The Book of Monasteries, by al-Shābushtī
Edited and translated by Hilary Kilpatrick (2023)

In Deadly Embrace: Arabic Hunting Poems, by Ibn al-Muʿtazz
Edited and translated by James E. Montgomery (2023)

The Divine Names, by ʿAfīf al-Dīn al-Tilimsānī
Edited and translated by Yousef Casewit (2023)

Bedouin Poets of the Nafūd Desert, by Khalaf Abū Zwayyid, ʿAdwān al-Hirbīd, and ʿAjlān ibn Rmāl
Edited and translated by Marcel Kurpershoek (2024)

The Rules of Logic, by Najm al-Dīn al-Kātibī
Edited and translated by Tony Street (2024)

Najm al-dīn al-Kātibī's al-Risālah al-Shamsiyyah: An Edition and Translation with Commentary, by Tony Street (2024)

English-only Paperbacks

Leg over Leg, by Aḥmad Fāris al-Shidyāq (2 volumes; 2015)

The Expeditions: An Early Biography of Muḥammad, by Maʿmar ibn Rāshid (2015)

The Epistle on Legal Theory: A Translation of al-Shāfiʿī's Risālah, by al-Shāfiʿī (2015)

The Epistle of Forgiveness, by Abū l-ʿAlāʾ al-Maʿarrī (2016)

The Principles of Sufism, by ʿĀʾishah al-Bāʿūniyyah (2016)

A Treasury of Virtues: Sayings, Sermons, and Teachings of ʿAlī, by al-Qāḍī al-Quḍāʿī with the *One Hundred Proverbs* attributed to al-Jāḥiẓ (2016)

The Life of Ibn Ḥanbal, by Ibn al-Jawzī (2016)

Mission to the Volga, by Ibn Faḍlān (2017)

Accounts of China and India, by Abū Zayd al-Sīrāfī (2017)

Consorts of the Caliphs: Women and the Court of Baghdad, by Ibn al-Sāʿī (2017)

A Hundred and One Nights (2017)

Disagreements of the Jurists: A Manual of Islamic Legal Theory, by al-Qāḍī al-Nuʿmān (2017)

What ʿĪsā ibn Hishām Told Us, by Muḥammad al-Muwayliḥī (2018)

War Songs, by ʿAntarah ibn Shaddād (2018)

The Life and Times of Abū Tammām, by Abū Bakr Muḥammad ibn Yaḥyā al-Ṣūlī (2018)

The Sword of Ambition, by ʿUthmān ibn Ibrāhīm al-Nābulusī (2019)

Brains Confounded by the Ode of Abū Shādūf Expounded: Volume One, by Yūsuf al-Shirbīnī (2019)

Brains Confounded by the Ode of Abū Shādūf Expounded: Volume Two, by Yūsuf al-Shirbīnī and *Risible Rhymes*, by Muḥammad ibn Maḥfūẓ al-Sanhūrī (2019)

The Excellence of the Arabs, by Ibn Qutaybah (2019)

Light in the Heavens: Sayings of the Prophet Muḥammad, by al-Qāḍī al-Quḍāʿī (2019)

Scents and Flavors: A Syrian Cookbook (2020)

Arabian Satire: Poetry from 18th-Century Najd, by Ḥmēdān al-Shwēʿir (2020)

In Darfur: An Account of the Sultanate and Its People, by Muḥammad al-Tūnisī (2020)

Arabian Romantic: Poems on Bedouin Life and Love, by Ibn Sbayyil (2020)

The Philosopher Responds: An Intellectual Correspondence from the Tenth Century, by Abū Ḥayyān al-Tawḥīdī and Abū ʿAlī Miskawayh (2021)

Impostures, by al-Ḥarīrī (2021)

The Discourses: Reflections on History, Sufism, Theology, and Literature—Volume One, by al-Ḥasan al-Yūsī (2021)

The Yoga Sutras of Patañjali, by Abū Rayḥān al-Bīrūnī (2022)

The Book of Charlatans, by Jamāl al-Dīn ʿAbd al-Raḥīm al-Jawbarī (2022)

The Book of Travels, by Ḥannā Diyāb (2022)

A Physician on the Nile: A Description of Egypt and Journal of the Famine Years, by ʿAbd al-Laṭīf al-Baghdādī (2022)

Kalīlah and Dimnah: Fables of Virtue and Vice, by Ibn al-Muqaffaʿ (2023)

Love, Death, Fame: Poetry and Lore from the Emirati Oral Tradition, by al-Māyidī ibn Ẓāhir (2023)

The Essence of Reality: A Defense of Philosophical Sufism, by ʿAyn al-Quḍāt (2023)

The Doctors' Dinner Party, by Ibn Buṭlān (2024)